SRA
Prescriptive English

A Basic Skills Program

A Division of The McGraw·Hill Companies

Columbus, Ohio

Credits

Formerly published as *Individual Corrective English*
by Edith H. Price, Flora B. Miller, and Irene Patchen Warner.

Cover Photo: Eclipse Studio

www.sra4kids.com

SRA/McGraw-Hill

A Division of The McGraw·Hill Companies

Send all inquiries to:
SRA/McGraw-Hill
8787 Orion Place
Columbus, OH 43240-4027

Printed in the United States of America.

ISBN 0-07-568958-8

2 3 4 5 6 7 8 9 QPD 06 05 04 03

Table of Contents

UNIT 2 Usage

UNIT 3 Mechanics

Name _____

Lesson 1

Grammar

Nouns: Common and Proper

A **noun** is a word that names a person, a place, or a thing. Two kinds of nouns are **common nouns** and **proper nouns.**

Rule	Example
Common nouns name one or more persons, places, or things.	woman, dogs, cities, park
Proper nouns name particular persons, places, or things.	Dale, Bailey, New York, Yosemite National Park

Underline the common nouns and circle the proper nouns in each sentence.

1. Pearl S. Buck was born in Hillsboro, West Virginia.

2. When she was an infant, Buck was taken to China, where her parents were missionaries.

3. There, Buck learned much about China.

4. When she returned to the United States, she wrote about China in many stories and published more than 100 books.

5. Her book *The Good Earth,* about a family in China, won the Pulitzer Prize.

6. She found homes for many children from Asia.

7. Buck went to Winhall, Vermont, to learn about making sugar from maple syrup.

8. She loved the snow, the woods, and the mountains.

9. In her home there, which she designed herself, her writing desk was at the window overlooking Stratton Mountain.

Extension
Write a paragraph about a trip you would like to take.

Count 1 point for each correct answer.

_____ **My Score**
35 Top Score

Lesson 2

NOUNS: Plurals

Rule	Example
To form the **plural** of most nouns, add –*s* to the singular.	cat, cats; bird, birds
To form the plural of nouns ending in *s, x, z, ch,* or *sh,* add –*es.*	dress, dresses; fox, foxes; ranch, ranches
For nouns ending in *y* after a vowel, add –*s.* For nouns ending in *y* after a consonant, change the *y* to *i* and add –*es.*	turkey, turkeys city, cities; sky, skies
To form the plural of some nouns ending in *f* or *fe,* add –*s.* For other nouns, change the *f* or *fe* to *v* and add –*es.*	chief, chiefs half, halves; wife, wives
To form the plural of some nouns ending in *o* after a vowel, add –*s.* For other nouns ending in *o* after a consonant, add –*es.*	radio, radios hero, heroes; potato, potatoes
To form the plural of some nouns, change the spelling. Some nouns keep the same form.	mouse, mice sheep, sheep

Write the plural of each noun. Use your dictionary if necessary.

1. nurse _____

2. watch _____

3. fly _____

4. turkey _____

5. trio _____

6. deer _____

7. gulf _____

8. tomato _____

9. shelf _____

10. child _____

Count 1 point for each correct answer.

_____ My Score

10 Top Score

Extension
Write a paragraph telling about a fun time you had recently with friends or family.

2

NOUNS: Possessives

> A **possessive noun** is a noun that shows ownership or possession.
>
> | Rule | Example |
> |------|---------|
> | To show possession in a singular noun, add an **apostrophe** and *s*. | Lisa saw a **bird's** nest. |
> | To show possession in a plural noun that does not end in *s*, add an **apostrophe** and *s*. | women, women's |
> | To show possession in a plural noun that ends in *s*, add an **apostrophe**. | boys, boys' |

Write the possessive form of each word.

1. mother _____

2. home _____

3. today _____

4. deer _____

5. Lisa _____

6. mothers _____

7. sheep _____

8. turkeys _____

9. schools _____

10. men _____

Write the possessive form of each word in parentheses.

11. A _____ nervous system is very complex. (person)

12. Although _____ studies have taught them much, they continue to study _____ nervous systems. (scientists) (people)

13. The nervous _____ central organ is the brain. (system)

14. The protection of our _____ nervous system is important. (bodies)

Count 1 point for each correct answer.

_____ **My Score**

15 Top Score

Extension
Write a paragraph about some of the people in your neighborhood (their family members, hobbies, and so on).

3

Lesson 4

Pronouns

A **pronoun** is a word used in place of a noun.

Marcia lost the ring Marcia had made.   →   Marcia lost the ring **she** had made.

Some commonly used pronouns are **I, my, mine, me, we, our, ours, us, he, him, his, she, her, hers, it, its, you, your, yours, they, their, theirs, them.**

Circle the pronouns in these sentences.

1. Leonardo da Vinci showed great ability in drawing even when he was a child.

2. When he turned 15, his father took him to study in Florence.

3. Da Vinci painted with such skill that his teacher put down his own paintbrushes and never picked them up again.

4. Before long, da Vinci set up his studio in the garden of his sponsor.

5. His painting *Mona Lisa,* with her small, knowing smile, is one of the most famous paintings in the world.

6. Today we can see the *Mona Lisa* in the Louvre Museum in Paris, France.

7. Da Vinci loved Florence so much that he would sometimes follow interesting townspeople for a whole day and then paint them from memory.

8. His careful observation helped him create paintings that were so realistic that they surprised viewers.

9. Besides painting, da Vinci also kept hundreds of notebooks in which he wrote down all kinds of new ideas.

10. He always wrote backward to keep his ideas secret.

Count 1 point for each correct answer.

_____ My Score
20 Top Score

Extension
Tell about an adventure you and your friends have had together.

Verbs: Principal Parts

A **verb** expresses action or state of being. All verbs have three principal parts: **present, past,** and **past participle.** They are used in forming almost all the tenses of the verb. Tense helps you tell when the action expressed by the verb takes place.

Rule	Example
The present and past parts may be used without a helping verb. With a helping verb such as **has, have, had, is, am, are, was,** or **were,** use the past participle.	I **do** exercises every morning. She **did** well on the test. We **have done** the art project. We **have** already **done** the art project.

Write the correct form of the verb in parentheses.

1. During most of human history, people have _____ in isolated groups. (live)

2. In the past, cities _____ far away from each other. (are)

3. People rarely _____ between them. (travel)

4. Interaction among different groups _____ a major effort. (take)

5. Infectious diseases in one area _____ among people in that area. (spread)

6. Epidemics, the rapid spread of diseases among many people, _____ rare. (are)

7. Only when different groups of people _____ others through trade, exploration, or war would epidemics _____ to other geographic regions. (meet) (spread)

8. In today's world, cars, trucks, trains, and airplanes have _____ slower-moving ships and caravans of the past. (replace)

9. As a result, epidemics happen more easily than they _____ in the past. (do)

Count 1 point for each correct answer.

_____ **My Score**
10 Top Score

Extension
Write a sentence with a helping verb and a main verb. Underline the helping verb and circle the main verb.

Lesson 6

Verbs: Verb Phrases

Rule	Example
A verb that is made of more than one word is called a **verb phrase**.	The magician **was doing** tricks. **Were** many people **watching**? She **has been studying** magic for years.

Circle the verb phrase in each sentence.

1. Gymnastics is considered a mixture of strength, agility, coordination, and balance tests.

2. The gymnasts must use standard equipment on which they can perform exercises that are marked by judges.

3. Men can compete in six events: rings, pommel horse, parallel bars, high bar, vault, and floor exercise.

4. Women can also complete in the vault and floor exercise, as well as on the beam and uneven parallel bars.

5. Many modern gymnasiums have provided other kinds of equipment that gymnasts can use for their practice.

6. Gymnasts can perform somersaults, cartwheels, and turns on the beam.

7. Exercises on the high bar must include nonstop swinging movements.

8. Performance is based on the difficulty of the exercises and how well they are performed.

9. Floor exercises are done on a marked area of 40 square feet.

10. Gymnasts are not allowed outside it.

11. Have you ever seen a gymnastics competition?

Count 1 point for each correct answer.

_____ **My Score**

15 Top Score

Extension
Write two sentences about your favorite hobby. Circle the verb phrases.

Name _____

Review Lessons 1–6

- Underline each common noun and circle each proper noun.

1. Christopher Columbus took his first trip across the Atlantic Ocean in 1492.

2. The trip took 70 days.

3. Charles Lindbergh flew from New York to Paris in 33 hours, 29 minutes, 30 seconds.

- Write the plural and plural possessive form of each noun.

4. child _____, _____

5. lady _____, _____

- Circle each pronoun.

6. Sedona Miller's creative mother made up her first name.

7. Sedona, Arizona, is named after her.

8. She loved this town and helped pioneer its development.

- Write the correct form of the verb in parentheses.

9. I _____ a great book yesterday. (read)

10. It _____ poems about baseball. (has)

11. It was _____ a high recommendation by the librarian. (gave)

- Circle the verb phrase in each sentence.

12. We will learn much about computers in school.

13. Have you ever used a computer?

Count 1 point for
each correct answer.

_____ **My Score**
25 Top Score

Direct Objects

Rule	Example
A **direct object** answers the question *what?* or *whom?* after an action verb.	Dale watched the **animals.** I saw my **brother.**

Circle the direct object.

1. From 1923 to 1929, the United States experienced great prosperity.

2. Many people made fortunes in the stock market.

3. Millions of Americans enjoyed better living conditions than ever before.

4. People also gained more time in which to spend their money.

5. Labor unions fought companies for a shorter workday.

6. At the same time, industries were producing new products that saved people time.

7. People called this exciting time the Roaring Twenties.

8. Young people danced the Charleston.

9. You quickly twist your knees in and out to do the Charleston.

10. Bands played jazz music full of striking rhythms and sounds.

11. Women wore shorter dresses.

12. Men wore long fur coats.

13. Many writers told stories about the Roaring Twenties.

14. F. Scott Fitzgerald called this period the greatest party in history.

15. Your great-grandparents might remember this time in American history.

Count 1 point for each correct answer.

_____ My Score

15 Top Score

Extension
Use each of these verbs in a sentence: *bought, saw, visited, shook, caught,* and *met.* Include an object of the verb in each sentence.

8

Lesson 8 UNIT 1: Grammar

Indirect Objects

Rule	Example
An **indirect object** is sometimes used between the verb and the direct object. It tells to whom or for whom something was done.	Pam gave **Linda** a book. The word *Linda* tells to whom the book was given.

Circle the indirect object.

1. A professional baseball player told our baseball team a lot about baseball at practice today.

2. The early settlers of the eighteenth century gave us the game of baseball.

3. I think we should give the early settlers a great deal of credit.

4. They gave us a great sport.

5. The umpire gives the batter three tries to hit the ball.

6. Our speaker told us the reason why only wooden bats are allowed in major league baseball.

7. The pitcher sends the batter fast and slow curve balls.

8. Some pitchers can pitch the batter a baseball at 100 miles per hour.

9. With a swing of the bat, the batter sends the fielders baseballs to catch.

10. A batter wants to try to give the fielders difficult balls to catch.

11. The fielders throw the basemen the ball as the batter runs to the base.

12. Our speaker played us a videotape of some famous baseball plays.

13. Good players can show you a lot of baseball tips.

14. We presented the speaker with a gift for coming to visit us.

15. Then he gave us an autographed baseball.

Count 1 point for each correct answer.

_____ My Score

15 Top Score

Extension
Write a thank-you note for a gift or favor you recently received.

Lesson 9

Adjectives and Adverbs: Comparative and Superlative

An **adjective** is a word that describes, points out, or numbers a noun or pronoun. An **adverb** is a word that tells how, when, where, or to what degree. Use the comparative form to compare two persons or things. Use the superlative form to compare more than two.

Rule	Example
For most one-syllable and some two-syllable adjectives and adverbs, add *–er* (comparative) or *–est* (superlative).	happy, happier, happiest soon, sooner, soonest
For most adjectives and adverbs of two or more syllables, use **more/less** (comparative) or **most/least** (superlative).	interesting, more interesting, most interesting politely, less politely, least politely
For some adjectives and adverbs, change the word.	good, better, best many, more, most well, better, best

Write the comparative and superlative forms of each adjective and adverb.

1. pretty _____

2. many _____

3. important _____

4. good _____

5. enjoyable _____

6. quickly _____

7. soon _____

8. quietly _____

9. slowly _____

10. hard _____

Count 1 point for each correct answer.

_____ **My Score**

20 Top Score

Extension
Tell your classmates about a book you have read recently.

10

Interjections and Conjunctions

Rule	Example
An **interjection** expresses strong feeling. **Hurrah, alas, oh,** and **ouch** are commonly used interjections. An interjection should usually be followed by an exclamation point.	**Hurrah!** Bill hit a home run!
A conjunction is a word that connects words or groups of words. **And, while, but, or, nor, because, if,** and **as** are commonly used conjunctions.	Sue **and** Ron went to the picnic.

Circle each interjection and add the needed exclamation points.

1. Look The sun is shining now!

2. Good Now we can play baseball!

3. Oh Rondell isn't here.

4. Ouch I stubbed my toe!

Circle each conjunction.

5. Rebekah and Dylan went to the picnic.

6. Marcia couldn't go because she was sick.

7. The picnickers will stay all day if it doesn't rain.

8. One group brought the sandwiches and lemonade.

9. Another group brought the cake and fruit.

10. Pierre and Debra fished while Kim and LeRoy hiked.

11. Debra said the fish weren't biting, but Pierre disagreed.

12. Pierre caught a bass and a catfish.

13. Debra and Pierre rested while LeRoy fried the fish.

Count 1 point for each correct answer.

_____ My Score
20 Top Score

Extension
Rewrite the paragraph from Lesson 2, adding interjections and exclamation points.

Lesson 11

Prepositions and Prepositional Phrases

Rule	Example
A **preposition** is a word that shows the relationship of a noun to another word in a sentence. A **prepositional phrase** is a group of words that begins with a preposition and ends with a noun or a pronoun. This noun or pronoun is called the **object of the preposition**.	object of the preposition The dog slept **under** the porch. prepositional phrase

above	between	for	of
at	by	from	to
before	during	into	with

In each sentence, underline the prepositional phrase once and the preposition twice. Use the list of prepositions above to help you.

1. The discomfort of early railroad travel was considerable.

2. The engine would look strange to you.

3. The cars for the passengers had uncomfortable seats.

4. Smoke blackened the faces of the passengers.

5. One day an accident happened to a locomotive.

6. Steam was escaping from the engine.

7. With great care, the engineer fastened the steam valve.

8. Steam mounted to the exploding point.

9. Parts of the engine were blown into a field.

Count 1 point for each correct answer.

_____ **My Score**
20 Top Score

Extension
Write three sentences with prepositional phrases. Underline the prepositional phrase once and the preposition twice.

Lesson **12**

Parts of Speech

Rule	Example
Every word in a sentence is a **part of speech.** The parts of speech include nouns, verbs, pronouns, adjectives, adverbs, prepositions, interjections, and conjunctions.	pron adv v prep adj adj n She quickly ran toward the finish line.

Above each word write the word's part of speech. Use *n* for *noun*, *v* for verb, *pron* for *pronoun*, *adj* for *adjective*, *adv* for *adverb*, *prep* for preposition, *conj* for *conjunction*, and *i* for *interjection*.

1. James Wilson was an important figure in American history.

2. Wilson was born in Scotland and then came to America.

3. He started his law practice in Pennsylvania.

4. Wilson married Rachel Bird, and they had six children.

5. Wilson was a great and convincing speaker.

6. He helped draft the Constitution.

Count 1 point for each correct answer.

_____ **My Score**
45 Top Score

Extension
Identify the parts of speech in the sentences you wrote for Lesson 11.

Review Lessons 7–12

- **Circle the direct objects.**

1. Deserts contain many plants.   2. These plants need little water.

- **Circle the indirect objects.**

3. The cashier told me the prices.

4. I will give you my address.

- **Write the correct form of each adjective or adverb in parentheses.**

5. The train ride was the _____ trip I have ever had. (enjoyable)

6. It travels _____ than I thought it would. (fast)

- **Circle each conjunction.**

7. Abbreviations and acronyms are shorter than a word or phrase.

8. *Pp.* and *Ave.* are common abbreviations.

9. NFL, NBA, and NHL are acronyms for sports leagues.

- **Underline the prepositional phrase once and the preposition twice.**

10. Come to the meeting in Classroom 12 at noon.

11. It is behind the cafeteria.

- **Above each word write the word's part of speech. Use *n* for *noun*, *v* for *verb*, *pron* for *pronoun*, *adj* for *adjective*, *adv* for *adverb*, *prep* for *preposition*, *conj* for *conjunction*, and *i* for *interjection*.**

12. Angel Falls in Venezuela is the highest waterfall.

13. Greenland is actually an island.

•Lesson 7 •Lesson 8 •Lesson 9 •Lesson 10 •Lesson 11 •Lesson 12

Count 1 point for each correct answer.

_____ My Score
30 Top Score

Sentences: Kinds

Rule	Example
A **declarative** sentence tells something. It should end with a period.	Max heard a strange sound.
An **interrogative** sentence asks a question. It should end with a question mark.	Was it the wind that he heard?
An **exclamatory** sentence expresses strong feeling. It should end with an exclamation mark.	How frightened the puppy was!
An **imperative** sentence expresses a command or a request. It should end with a period.	Come to the window and see for yourself.

Write _D_ before each declarative sentence, _Q_ before each interrogative sentence, _E_ before each exclamatory sentence, and _I_ before each imperative sentence. Place the correct mark at the end of each sentence.

1. _____ Did you know that several women had a part in the Alamo battle of 1836

2. _____ Suzanna Dickerson was 18 when she cared for the sick and wounded during the battle

3. _____ What a brave woman she was

4. _____ Another little-known person of the Alamo battle is Andrea Candelaria

5. _____ Imagine how she felt when the battle erupted

Count 1 point for each correct answer.

_____ **My Score**
10 Top Score

Extension
Write a declarative, interrogative, exclamatory, and imperative sentence about a recent experience.

Sentences: Recognizing

Rule	Example
A **sentence** is a group of words that expresses a complete thought. Always capitalize the first word of a sentence.	Many people live in Milltown. Is Milltown in Pennsylvania?

Write *Yes* before each group of words that is a sentence. Circle the letter that should be a capital. Put the correct end mark at the end of each sentence. Write *No* before the other groups.

1. _____ where is Milltown

2. _____ because New York is not far from Philadelphia

3. _____ Pennsylvania was a colony of England

4. _____ has a large river but no seacoast

5. _____ most of the people live in towns and cities

6. _____ one of the leading industrial states

7. _____ its farms produce much food for the cities

8. _____ the first oil well in the United States was drilled in Pennsylvania

9. _____ drilled near Titusville in 1859

10. _____ Pittsburgh is a great manufacturing center

Count 1 point for each correct answer.

_____ **My Score**
20 Top Score

Extension
Write three complete sentences about a state you would like to see other than your own. Tell what you would like to see.

Lesson 15

Sentences: Complete Subject and Simple Subject

Rule	Example
The **complete subject** is made of all the words in a sentence that name or describe the person, place, or thing talked about.	**A happy crowd from our town** gathered at the entrance.
The **simple subject** is the main word of the complete subject and is usually a noun or a pronoun.	A happy **crowd** from our town gathered at the entrance.

In each sentence, underline the complete subject and circle the simple subject.

1. A guided tour of Carlsbad Caverns is a wonderful experience.

2. Many tourists visit Carlsbad Caverns in southern New Mexico.

3. The cool, damp air of the caverns makes it wise to take a jacket.

4. You walk down the steps into the caverns.

5. The mysterious beauties of nature unfold around you.

6. Stone icicles hang from the ceiling.

7. They are called stalactites.

8. Clear and quiet lakes can be seen below the paths.

9. Numerous bats fly from the caves in search of flying insects.

10. The bats cling to the ceilings of the cave during the day.

Count 1 point for each correct answer.

_____ My Score
20 Top Score

Extension
Using complete subjects, write a paragraph about a fun time you have had with your class or family.

Sentences: Complete Predicate and Simple Predicate

Rule	Example
The **complete predicate** is made of the verb and all the other words that tell something about the subject.	The bees **swarmed around the old hive.**
The **simple predicate** is the verb or verb phrase in the complete predicate.	The bees **swarmed** around the old hive.

Underline the complete predicate and circle the simple predicate.

1. Honeybees look for a new hive when their old hive becomes crowded.

2. A band of scouts hunts for a new home.

3. They may fly great distances in their search.

4. Thousands of bees swarm from the hive.

5. They wait for reports from the scouts.

6. These scouting bees can describe the various spots by dancing.

7. The dance tells where the place is located.

8. Bees are always working around the hive.

9. The worker bees gather nectar for honey.

10. Some of the workers build the honeycomb.

11. Some of them must feed the baby bees.

12. Others fan air into the hive.

13. Still others guard the hive.

14. They sting any approaching enemy.

15. Some worker bees live only a few weeks.

Count 1 point for each correct answer.

_____ My Score
30 Top Score

Extension
Write a paragraph about how you make your favorite lunch. Give details.

Lesson 17

Sentences: Simple and Compound

Rule	Example
A **simple sentence** is made of only one subject and predicate.	The Andersons will be here soon.
In a simple sentence, both the subject and the predicate may be compound.	**Presidents Washington** and **Lincoln** were born in February. We **biked** and **rode** sleds on vacation.
A **compound sentence** is made of two or more simple sentences put together.	**My sister and I visited Sue,** and **we had a great time.**

Write SS for *simple sentence* and CS for *compound sentence*. Circle the simple subjects and underline the simple predicates in each sentence.

1. _____ Climate is the average weather of an area and is the subject of study for many scientists.

2. _____ Temperature is measured over a long period of time.

3. _____ Cool, dry desert and humid tropics are two kinds of climate.

4. _____ Weather and climate are constant forces in our lives, and they affect how we live.

5. _____ Earth's movement also affects weather changes and seasons.

6. _____ You can write to Mrs. Duntov, a meteorologist, and she may send you some interesting facts about climate.

Count 1 point for each correct answer.

_____ My Score
25 Top Score

Extension
Rewrite the paragraph you wrote in Lesson 16 using compound sentences.

Sentences: Run-Ons

Rule	Example
A sentence should have only one thought.	Shawna starts school in August.
A **run-on sentence** is two or more sentences written as though they were one sentence. The two sentences have no end marks between them.	I believe our school starts then too when does yours start?
Run-on sentences need to be separated by end marks and have capital letters at the beginning of the new sentences.	I believe our school starts then too. When does yours start?

The paragraph below has been written as though it were several long sentences. Read these sentences to find the beginning and the end of each sentence. Circle the letters that should be capital letters. Put the correct mark at the end of each sentence.

Basketball was invented in 1891 a clergyman, Dr. James Naismith, nailed a peach basket to the balcony at each end of a gym. The object of the game is to throw the ball into the basket basketball is usually played indoors with five players on each side the players throw and bounce the ball but cannot carry or kick it. There are many tall players in basketball one of the greatest players of all time, Michael Jordan, retired in 1999 he helped the Chicago Bulls win six NBA championships. He was selected Most Valuable Player in the NBA five times there are now two conferences and four divisions in professional basketball you may want to visit the Naismith Memorial Basketball Hall of Fame in Springfield, Massachusetts

Count 1 point for each correct answer.

_____ **My Score**

15 Top Score

Extension
Proofread some of your recent writing. Make sure you don't have any run-on sentences.

Name _____

- Write *D* before each declarative sentence, *Q* before each interrogative sentence, and *I* before each imperative sentence. Place the correct mark at the end of each sentence.

1. _____ Light is a form of energy that travels in rays

2. _____ Did you know they can travel at a speed of 186,000 miles per second

- Write *Yes* before each group of words that is a sentence. Circle the letter that should be a capital. Put the correct end mark at the end of each sentence. Write *No* before the other groups.

3. _____ it also moves through materials like water and glass

- Underline the complete subject and circle the simple subject.

4. Vibrating objects can create sound.

5. The vibrations travel through the air in waves.

- Underline the complete predicate and circle the simple predicate.

6. Sound waves have to have something through which to move.

7. Air is usually what the waves travel through.

8. Sound can also travel through water, wood, glass, and other materials.

- Write *SS* for *simple sentence* or *CS* for *compound sentence*. Circle each simple subject and underline each simple predicate.

9. _____ Laughing, tapping, singing, and humming are noises, and they can be measured in decibels.

• Lesson 13 • Lesson 14 • Lesson 15 • Lesson 16 • Lesson 17

Count 1 point for each correct answer.

_____ **My Score**
25 Top Score

UNIT 1: Grammar

Cumulative Review   Unit 1

•Lesson 1   **Underline each common noun and circle each proper noun.**

   1. Explorers searched for the legendary southern continent for centuries.

   2. In 1768, James Cook landed his ship in Botany Bay.

•Lessons 2, 3   **Write the plural and plural possessive forms of each noun.**

   3. land _____ _____   4. ax _____ _____

•Lesson 4   **Circle each pronoun.**

   5. Explorers founded the first settlement in Australia, which they named New South Wales, in 1788.

   6. At first, it was a prison colony, but it would later become a thriving democracy.

•Lessons 5, 6   **Write the correct form of the verb in parentheses after the sentence.**

   7. Australia's first inhabitants _____ aborigines. (are)

   8. Europeans _____ not find the gold that they came in search of. (do)

   9. Instead, they _____ interesting animals like kangaroos and koalas. (find)

•Lessons 1–12   **Above each word write the word's part of speech. Use *n* for *noun*, *v* for *verb*, *pron* for *pronoun*, *adj* for *adjective*, *adv* for *adverb*, *prep* for *preposition*, *conj* for *conjunction*, and *i* for *interjection*.**

  10. Elizabeth Veale helped build the future of the colony.

  11. She was married to a successful sheep owner named John Macarthur.

  12. Her husband spent much of his time outside the colony.

  13. As a result, she was often responsible for their estate in Australia.

  14. She did this job very successfully and helped establish the production of wool as an important industry in Australia.

Cumulative Review

•Lesson 13

Write *D* before each declarative sentence, *Q* before each interrogative sentence, *E* before each exclamatory sentence, and *I* before each imperative sentence. Place the correct mark at the end of each sentence.

15. _____ What type of government was found in New South Wales

16. _____ The English discovered fertile land on the east coast of Australia

17. _____ They also found a dry region in the middle of the continent

18. _____ Imagine the aborigines' surprise when they saw the explorers

19. _____ It was shocking

•Lesson 15

Underline the complete subject and circle the simple subject.

20. For decades, the jails of England had been overcrowded.

21. Some prisoners were sent to work in the American colonies.

22. After the American Revolution, the English needed a new place to send their convicts.

•Lesson 16

Underline the complete predicate, and circle the simple predicate.

23. A convict is a person who has been found guilty of a crime.

24. The first ship carrying convicts arrived in Australia in 1788.

25. The oldest convict was 82.

26. The youngest was only nine years old.

Count 1 point for each correct answer.

_____ My Score
100 Top Score

UNIT 1 Inventory

Underline the common nouns and circle the proper nouns in each sentence. Lesson 1

1. Schillings are used as currency in Austria.

2. In Armenia, the dram is used.

3. Comoros, which is a group of islands between Madagascar and Africa, uses francs.

Write the plural and plural possessive forms of each noun. Lessons 2, 3

4. story _____ _____

5. language _____ _____

Circle each pronoun. Lesson 4

6. Colds are the most common illnesses we get.

7. Children often catch colds from their friends.

8. You cannot catch a cold by going outside without a coat, but washing your hands is a good way to avoid catching a virus.

Write the correct form of the verb in parentheses after the sentence. Lesson 5

9. Colds are _____ by viruses. (cause)

10. I _____ a cold that lasted three weeks. (have)

Circle the direct object. Lesson 7

11. Medicines do not cure colds.

12. Staying home will not cure your cold.

13. Does cold weather cause viruses?

Circle the indirect object. Lesson 8

14. Eating too many sweets gave me a cavity.

15. The dentist told us the facts about brushing.

16. I will show you the proper technique.

Above each word write the word's part of speech. Use *n* for *noun*, *v* for *verb*, *pron* for *pronoun*, *adj* for *adjective*, *adv* for *adverb*, *prep* for *preposition*, *conj* for *conjunction*, and *i* for *interjection*. Lesson 12

17. A person with allergies is very sensitive to normally harmless things.

18. It could be a food you eat.

19. See a doctor immediately for severe allergic reactions.

Write *Yes* before each group of words that is a sentence. Circle the letter that should be a capital. Put the correct end mark at the end of each sentence. Write *No* before the other groups. Lesson 14

20. _____ what is asthma

21. _____ causes difficulty in breathing

22. _____ many things can start an asthma attack

Count 1 point for each correct answer.

_____ **My Score**

60 Top Score

24

Name _____

Lesson 19

Contractions

Rule	Example
A **contraction** is a shortened form of two words that leaves out one or more letters. An **apostrophe** is used to show where the letter or letters have been left out.	**you're** (you are) **isn't** (is not) **I'm** (I am) **won't** (will not) **let's** (let us) **doesn't** (does not)

Write the contractions of these words.

1. let us _____

2. you are _____

3. she will _____

4. was not _____

5. it has _____

6. cannot _____

7. had not _____

8. that is _____

Write a contraction made from the words in the parentheses.

9. Many people _____ know much about the human heart. (do not)

10. _____ a fist-sized organ _____ divided into halves. (It is) (that is)

11. _____ the upper atrium and lower ventricle. (They are)

12. The heart _____ get tired because it rests between beats. (does not)

13. If it _____ for the heart, we _____ be able to live. (were not, would not)

Count 1 point for each correct answer.

_____ My Score

15 Top Score

Extension
Review a piece of your recent writing. Replace some words with contractions.

25

Pronouns: Subjective Case

A pronoun is often used with a noun or another pronoun as part of the subject of a sentence. The subject names whom or what the sentence is about.

Rule	Example
When a pronoun is used as a subject, the forms **I, he, she, it, you, we,** or **they** should be used.	**We** were invited to the farm.
In speaking of yourself and someone else together, always speak of yourself last.	Carla and **I** had fun at the farm.
To help you decide which pronoun to use, try using one pronoun alone.	**Me** had fun at the farm. (incorrect) **I** had fun at the farm. (correct)

Circle the correct word or word groups.

1. Carla and **I me** went to Kansas to visit her grandparents' farm.

2. **Us We** learned that it had been homesteaded by their ancestors in the 1800s.

3. **They Them** had come from Germany to settle there.

4. **Carla and I Carla and me** saw the place where **them they** had dug their first well.

5. When **us we** saw her grandfather's new combine with a television in it, **us we** appreciated how hard the early settlers had worked!

6. **Them They** also survived such hardships as prairie fires, unpredictable weather, grasshoppers, and locusts.

7. Her grandmother and **us we** rode in the original wagon pulled by a horse.

8. **I Me** really enjoyed learning about farming in the Great Plains.

Count 1 point for each correct answer.

_____ My Score

10 Top Score

Extension
Write a paragraph about an adventure you and a friend would like to have. Proofread for correct pronoun use.

Lesson 21

Pronouns: Objective Case

A pronoun is often used with a noun or another pronoun as part of the direct object, the indirect object, or the object of a preposition.

A **direct object** answers the question *what?* or *whom?* after an action verb.

An **indirect object** answers the question *to whom? for whom? to what?* or *for what?* after an action verb.

The **object of a preposition** is the noun or pronoun that ends a prepositional phrase.

Rule	Example
When a pronoun is used as an object, the forms **me, him, her, it, you, us,** or **them** should be used.	Ana and Carlos called Jorge and **me.** They wanted to play tennis with **him** and **me.**
To help you decide whether to use the subject or the object form of the pronoun, try using one pronoun alone.	Ana and Carlos called **me.** They wanted to play tennis with **him.** They wanted to play tennis with **me.**

Circle the correct word.

1. Ana and Carlos often play tennis with Jorge and **I   me.**

2. We play on a court with a low net between **us   we.**

3. My uncle gave **I   me** a new racket for my birthday.

4. He told **I   me** it had a graphite frame.

5. Ana and Carlos told **he   him** and **I   me** how tennis balls are made from a rubber ball covered with a mixture of wool and artificial fibers.

6. Ana served the ball to **I   me,** and I returned it to **her   she.**

7. Ana and Carlos hit the ball right to **us   we.**

8. We didn't do as well hitting it back to **them   they.**

Count 1 point for each correct answer.

_____ **My Score**

10 Top Score

Extension
Write a paragraph about a time someone gave you a gift or did you a favor. Proofread for correct pronoun use.

Lesson 22

Pronouns or Contractions

Rule	Example
Use **your, its, whose,** and **theirs** as possessive pronouns. Never use an apostrophe in a possessive pronoun.	The green tent is **theirs**.
You're, it's, who's and **there's** are contractions for **you are, it is, who is,** and **there is.**	**There's** a question about **who's** supposed to bring the wood.

Circle the correct word.

1. I heard   **you're   your**   traveling with us to the Northeast this summer.

2. **Who's   Whose**   idea was it?

3. The Green Mountains of Vermont are beautiful, and   **there   they're**   a great place for hiking.

4. **Theirs   There's**   a trail called the Long Trail that runs the length of Vermont.

5. **It's   Its**   one of our favorite places.

6. **Theirs   There's**   a campground we always visit, too.

7. **You're   Your**   campsite is right next to a lake.

8. You will love   **it's   its**   clear, cool water.

9. Then   **you're   your**   trip takes you to New York City.

10. **Theirs   There's**   a museum at Ellis Island that we should visit.

11. The Chungs always go there;   **it's   its**   a favorite of   **theirs   there's.**

12. **There   They're**   going to the Metropolitan Museum of Art this year.

13. **Who's   Whose**   ready to go with us?

14. **You're   Your**   going to love this part of our country.

Count 1 point for each correct answer.

_____ **My Score**

15 Top Score

Extension
Write three sentences using *your* and three sentences using *you're*.

28

Lesson 23

Pronouns: Who/Whom

Rule	Example
In questions, use **who** for subjects.	**Who** was at the door? **Who** is the subject of the verb **was.**
In questions, use **whom** for the direct object.	**Whom** did you see? **Whom** is the direct object of the verb **see.**
In questions, use **whom** for the object of a preposition.	To **whom** did you send the invitations? **Whom** is the object of the preposition **to.**

Circle the correct word.

1. **Who Whom**   should I ask?
2. **Who Whom**   will be the next president?
3. By **who whom** was *For* **Who Whom** *the Bell Tolls* written?
4. **Who Whom**   is going?
5. **Who Whom**   do you think is responsible for that decision?
6. **Who Whom**   left his books here?
7. To **who whom**   shall I report?
8. **Who Whom**   do you know in San Diego?
9. **Who Whom**   needs a ride home?
10. For **who whom**   are these documents?
11. **Who Whom**   does the manager want?
12. **Who Whom**   do you think broke the vase?
13. **Who Whom**   should we choose?
14. **Who Whom**   won the game?

Count 1 point for each correct answer.

_____ **My Score**

15 Top Score

Extension
Write two sentences using *who* and two sentences using *whom.*

Lesson 24

Pronouns: Redundancies

Rule	Example	
The pronouns **she, he, it,** and **they** are used in place of names. They should not be used after names.	Correct:	**Marsha** went to the zoo.
	Incorrect:	**Marsha she** went to the zoo.

Do not add **here** or **there** after **this, that, these,** or **those.**	**Correct**	**Incorrect**
	this	this here
	those	those there

Cross out the pronouns that are not needed.

1. Learning about space it is important and exciting.

2. Observing from Earth, sending instruments into space, and sending people into space they are ways we can study space.

3. Every space flight it begins with a rocket.

4. Rockets they are basically tubes filled with fuel that is ignited.

5. These here gases escape through the open end of the rocket.

6. Those there gases create a force that gives the rocket power to launch into space.

7. Rockets they can be used only one time.

8. John Glenn he became the first U.S. astronaut to orbit Earth.

9. In 1968, the United States spacecraft *Apollo 8* it orbited the moon ten times and returned safely to this here planet.

Count 1 point for each correct answer.

_____ **My Score**
10 Top Score

Extension
Review a piece of your recent writing. Proofread it for pronoun redundancies.

Review Lessons 19–24

- Write the contractions of these words.

1. you will _____

2. it has _____

3. it is _____

4. she would _____

- Circle the correct word or word groups.

5. **Her She** and **I me** will be happy to help.

6. **He and she Him and her** are flying to town.

7. My mother asked **I me** to make dinner.

8. I made a roast for **us we.**

9. Bill set the table for Mother and **I me.**

10. **Who's Whose** bringing the hot dogs to the picnic?

11. I think **you're your** bringing them.

12. **Theirs There's** a nice, cool breeze.

13. I like **it's its** refreshing smell.

14. **Who Whom** was at the door?

15. By **who whom** is your favorite song?

16. Do you know **who whom** is next in line?

- Cross out the pronouns that are not needed.

17. Harry S. Truman he was born on May 8, 1884, in Lamar, Missouri.

18. Truman he married Bess Wallace.

19. The couple they had one daughter.

•Lesson 19 •Lessons 20–23 •Lesson 24

Count 1 point for each correct answer.

_____ **My Score**
20 Top Score

Lesson 25

Pronouns: Reflexive

Reflexive pronouns refer back to the subject of the sentence.

Rule	Example
Use **herself** when the subject of the sentence is a **female**.	Brenda **herself** suggested the hiking trip.
Use **himself** when the subject of the sentence is a **male**.	Joe brought enough fruit for **himself**.
Use **themselves** when you speak of more than one **person**.	The four friends enjoyed **themselves**.
Do **not** use **hisself, theirself,** or **theirselves**.	

Write *herself, himself,* or *themselves* in each blank.

1. Jim used a calculator to check _____ on his math answers.

2. She taught _____ the guitar.

3. They went to the art museum by _____.

4. Maria bought _____ a jacket with her babysitting money.

5. The students _____ raised the money for the party.

Circle the correct word.

6. The four friends planned the hike by **theirselves   themselves.**

7. José designed the float **himself   hisself.**

8. He did **himself   hisself** a favor by going to bed early.

9. May they help **theirselves   themselves** to dessert?

10. They assigned **theirselves   themselves** three lessons per night.

Count 1 point for each correct answer.

_____ **My Score**

10 Top Score

Extension
Write one sentence each with *herself, himself,* and *themselves.*

Lesson 26

This, That, These, Those, Them

Rule	Example
Use **this, that, these,** and **those** as adjectives to point out persons or things about which you are speaking. Use **this** and **that** with singular nouns and **these** and **those** with plural nouns.	I like **this** kind of book. **Those** books look interesting.
Use **them** as a pronoun to stand for the names of persons or things. Do not use **them** as an adjective to point out persons or things.	Incorrect: I will buy them books. Correct: I will buy **them.**

Circle the correct word.

1. In **this these** lesson, we will learn about plants.

2. There are two types of tissues that transport food and water throughout plants, and we will study **this these** types of tissues.

3. **Those Them**   two types are vascular and nonvascular.

4. **This These** plants are flowering plants, but **those them** are nonflowering.

5. Did you know that **this these** plant is called an annual?

6. **This These** kinds of plants grow from a seed, produce flowers, create new seeds, and die all in one growing season.

7. **This These** tomatoes, beans, and potatoes are annuals.

8. Can you guess which type **this these** evergreens are?

9. **This These** tree is called a perennial because it lives more than two seasons.

Extension
Tell your classmates about a kind of music you like and why.

Count 1 point for each correct answer.

_____ My Score
10 Top Score

Verbs: Irregular Past Tense

Rule	Example		
An irregular verb forms its past and past participle in some way other than by adding *-ed* or *-d* to the base form.	**present**	**past**	**past participle**
	be	was, were	been
	become	became	become
	fly	flew	flown

Complete the chart. Check your dictionary if needed.

	present	past	past participle
1.	break	_____	_____
2.	bring	_____	_____
3.	draw	_____	_____
4.	know	_____	_____
5.	lead	_____	_____
6.	ring	_____	_____
7.	swim	_____	_____
8.	throw	_____	_____

Write the correct form of the verb in parentheses.

9. *Profiles in Courage* _____ a Pulitzer Prize in 1957. (win)

10. It _____ about eight great Americans who had _____ against popular opinion in matters in which they _____ strongly. (is) (stand) (feel)

Count 1 point for each correct answer.

_____ My Score

20 Top Score

Extension
Write one sentence each using *ride, rode,* and *ridden.*

Lesson 28

Subject/Verb Agreement: *Be, Do,* and *Have* Verbs

Rule	Example
Use **is, was, has,** and **does** with a singular subject.	Mini **is** bringing pictures of Bryce Canyon.
Use **are, were, have,** and **do** with a plural subject and with the word *you* when used as a subject.	Mini and Winona **are** eager to tell about their trip. You **have** to hear about it.
Use **am, was, have,** and **do** with the word *I* when used as a subject.	I **am** looking forward to it.

Circle the correct word.

1. **Has Have** you ever visited a national park?

2. National parks **are is** lands our government **has have** set aside to protect.

3. They **are is** a legacy for all Americans to enjoy.

4. A legacy **are is** something we **has have** received from the past that we want to pass on to the future.

5. The world's first national park **were was** Yellowstone, established in 1872.

6. Denali National Park in Alaska **was were** established in 1980.

7. I **am are** reading a book about the Everglades.

8. It **are is** called *The Everglades: River of Grass.*

9. Everglades National Park **are is** a huge swamp in Florida.

10. **Do Does** your family ever travel to national parks?

11. We **was were** in Yosemite National Park in California last summer.

12. **Do Does** you see why it **are is** important to protect wild places?

Count 1 point for each correct answer.

_____ My Score

15 Top Score

Extension
Discuss with your classmates which television programs are class favorites. List the reasons that these shows are popular.

Lesson 29

Subject/Verb Agreement: *Be* Verbs with *There*

Rule	Example
When a sentence begins with the word **there,** look for the subject after the verb. If the subject is singular, use **there is** or **there was.**	**There is** a digital watch on the market today.
If the subject is plural, use **there are** or **there were.**	**There are** several models from which to choose.

Circle the correct word.

1. There **are is** four times zones in the continental United States.

2. There **are is** one hour's difference between one time zone and the next.

3. There **are is** 24 time zones in the world.

4. There **was were** sundials in ancient times to tell time.

5. There **are is** a pole at the center of the sundial.

6. There **are is** markings to tell time by the position of the pole's shadow.

7. There **was were** no way to tell time if there **was were** no sunshine.

8. There **was were** many beautiful sundials made by early civilizations.

9. There **was were** even little sundials that people carried with them.

10. There **are is** sandglasses, or hourglasses, in use today.

11. There **was were** clocks being made toward the end of the thirteenth century.

12. There **was were** no early clocks that were very accurate.

13. There **are is** many ways to keep time today.

14. There **are is** watches that give the date as well as the time.

Count 1 point for each correct answer.

_____ My Score

15 Top Score

Extension
Discuss with your classmates the different ways in which time has been measured. Make a list of things that measure time.

Subject/Verb Agreement: Collective Nouns

Rule	Example
A **collective noun** takes a **singular verb** when the group is acting together.	Our **team is** winning. The **herd was** taken to the meadow.
A **collective noun** takes a **plural verb** when the individuals of the group are acting separately.	The **team have** voted on the mascot. The **crew are** wearing their summer uniforms now.
Sometimes a **collective noun** is **separated** from the verb.	The **crew** of sailors **is** waiting for its orders. The **jury** of citizens **sits** to the left of the judge.

Circle the correct verb.

1. Our school soccer team **work works** hard at every practice.

2. Before the first game, the team **vote votes** for a new captain.

3. On game days, the team **wear wears** their uniforms with pride.

4. The audience of parents **cheer cheers** for every goal.

5. The team **celebrate celebrates** a victory by getting pizza.

6. Our city's orchestra **is are** one of the best in the country.

7. The orchestra **plays play** at important events.

8. The orchestra **practices practice** three times a week.

9. After a concert, the orchestra **packs pack** their instruments.

10. Then the orchestra **goes go** to their homes.

Count 1 point for
each correct answer.   _____ My Score
                              10 Top Score

Extension
Write a paragraph about something you
have seen a group do, such as a crowd at a
football game.

Review Lessons 25–30

- **Write *herself, himself,* or *themselves* in each blank.**

1. The four friends planned the hike by _____.

2. Sara marked the trail _____.

3. Eduardo led the group _____ for the first part of the trail.

- **Circle the correct word.**

4. They like **this   these** kinds of books.

5. Have you read any of **them   those** books?

- **Write the correct form of the verb in parentheses.**

6. My cousin has _____ his own car. (buy)

7. Have you _____ a cold? (catch)

- **Circle the correct word.**

8. I **am   is** a sophomore.

9. He **has   have**   seen the movie.

10. They **was   were** going to Canada.

11. **Do   Does**   they vote every year?

- **Circle the correct word.**

12. The herd of antelope **are   is**   on display at the zoo.

13. Her choice of words **was   were**   vast for a three-year-old.

14. A bunch of grapes often **make   makes**   a colorful centerpiece.

15. This book of poems **was   were**   illustrated by a famous artist.

Count 1 point for
each correct answer.

_____ **My Score**
15 Top Score

Lesson 31

Verbs: Dangling Modifiers

Rule	Example
A **dangling modifier** fails to refer logically to any word in the sentence. Dangling modifiers are usually introductory word groups that suggest but do not clearly name the person or thing performing the action.	While watching television, the doorbell rang. (A doorbell cannot watch television.)
To correct a **dangling modifier**, supply a word for it to modify sensibly or change the participle to a main verb and add a subject.	While watching television, **we** heard the doorbell ring. While **we were watching** television, the doorbell rang.

Revise these sentences to correct the dangling participles.

1. Reading in the library, the siren of a passing ambulance distracted me.

   _____

2. To get a better view of the stage, our seats were changed.

   _____

3. While in the bowling alley, the car was stolen.

   _____

4. While only in elementary school, my father taught me some difficult chess moves.

   _____

5. While sitting in the high chair, I was afraid the baby would fall out.

   _____

Count 1 point for each correct answer.

_____ My Score

5 Top Score

Extension
Write a sentence with a dangling modifier. Exchange with a partner to correct.

Lesson **32**   UNIT 2: Usage

Verb Forms: Rang/Rung, Sang/Sung, Sank/Sunk, Drank/Drunk, Ate/Eaten, Swam/Swum

Rule	Example
Use **rang, sang, sank, drank, ate,** and **swam** alone.	Carol and Ron **sang** a duet.
With helping verbs such as **is, am, are, was, were, has, have,** or **had,** use **rung, sung, sunk, drunk, eaten,** and **swum.**	They **have sung** at several dances.

Circle the correct word.

1. Has the doorbell **rang   rung**   again?

2. I thought it **rang   rung**   a moment ago.

3. Soon the guests had **ate   eaten**   some sandwiches.

4. They **drank   drunk**   glasses of cold lemonade.

5. All the sandwiches were **ate   eaten.**

6. Some guests have **ate   eaten**   and **drank   drunk**   all they can.

7. Some people had **swam   swum**   in the pool before they **ate   eaten.**

8. Liza had **swam   swum**   across the pool five times.

9. Nami **swam   swum**   with Liza.

10. Liza has **swam   swum**   farther than Jack has **swam   swum.**

11. They watched as an old tube **sank   sunk**   beneath the surface of the pool.

12. It had **sank   sunk**   to the bottom of the pool.

Count 1 point for each correct answer.

_____ **My Score**
15 Top Score

Extension
Write six sentences with words studied in this lesson.

Verb Forms: Saw/Seen, Went/Gone, Did/Done, Came/Come, Took/Taken

Rule	Example
Use **saw, went, did, came,** and **took** alone.	Alberto and Yolanda **saw** some African art.
With a helping verb such as **is, am, are, was, were, has, have,** or **had,** use **seen, gone, done, come,** and **taken.**	They **had seen** many interesting things at the museum.

Circle the correct word.

1. Alberto and Yolanda have **gone went** to the museum.

2. They **gone went** to see portraits by Pierre Renoir and Mary Cassatt.

3. They **taken took** the bus.

4. They have also **gone went** to see a special exhibit that has just **came come** to the museum.

5. The museum is showing paintings that were **done did** by Picasso.

6. It **taken took** Alberto and Yolanda only 15 minutes to find the museum.

7. They have **came come** 20 minutes before opening time.

8. "We **came come** early," said Yolanda when she **saw seen** locked doors.

9. Alberto and Yolanda **saw seen** many interesting pieces of art at the show.

10. They had never **saw seen** landscapes by Jan Vermeer or Georgia O'Keeffe.

11. They were thrilled that they **saw seen** Wassily Kandinsky's abstracts.

12. They thought the museum had **did done** a wonderful job at displaying Picasso's works.

13. They were glad they had **came come** to this great museum.

Count 1 point for each correct answer.

_____ My Score

15 Top Score

Extension
Write a paragraph about a place you have visited, using some words studied in this lesson.

Lesson 34

Verb Forms: Rode/Ridden, Spoke/Spoken, Wrote/Written, Gave/Given, Chose/Chosen, Broke/Broken

Rule	Example
Use **rode, spoke, wrote, gave, chose,** and **broke** alone.	Sue **gave** the story a good ending.
Use **ridden, spoken, written, given, chosen,** and **broken** with helpers such as **is, am, are, was, were, has, have,** or **had.**	Sue **has chosen** a title for her story. The story **was written** well.

Circle the correct word.

1. *Heaven,* which won the Coretta Scott King Award, was **written wrote** by Angela Johnson.

2. The winner is **choose chosen** for works that promote the cause of peace.

3. Maya Angelou **spoke spoken** about her books at a conference last weekend.

4. We were glad she **chose chosen** to attend.

5. I heard she had **broke broken** her arm, but that wasn't true.

6. Has she **gave given** you her autograph?

7. We had **ridden rode** more than 600 miles to see her.

8. The conference organizers had **chose chosen** a large hotel.

9. She **spoke spoken** about her interesting life.

10. Each of us was **given gave** a copy of her latest book.

Count 1 point for each correct answer.

_____ My Score
10 Top Score

Extension
Write a paragraph about a speech you have given or a paper you have written. Use some words learned in this lesson.

Lesson **35**   UNIT 2: Usage

Verb Forms: Ran/Run, Began/Begun, Stole/Stolen, Froze/Frozen, Wore/Worn, Tore/Torn

Rule	Example
Use *ran, began, stole, froze, wore,* and *tore* alone.	The dog **ran** away.
With helping verbs such as *is, am, are, was, were, has, have,* or *had,* use *run, begun, stolen, frozen, worn,* and *torn*.	The dog **had run** away.

Circle the correct word.

1. Our trip to Canada **began   begun**   early.

2. Snow **began   begun**   to fall as we drove north.

3. The snow soon **froze   frozen**   on the windshield of our car.

4. We **ran   run**   the car to the side of the road.

5. The wind **tore   torn**   at the trees' branches.

6. We were glad we had **wore   worn**   our warmest coats.

7. A man **ran   run**   up to the side of our car.

8. He told us the storm had **tore   torn**   down a bridge just ahead.

9. We **began   begun**   to think we should **ran   run**   back to Ann Arbor.

10. The man told us about a road that was not **froze   frozen.**

11. He gave us directions because he said the road sign had been **stole   stolen.**

12. We started again and saw that the road ahead was **wore   worn**   but passable.

13. Soon we had **ran   run**   across another bridge that was not **froze   frozen.**

Count 1 point for each correct answer.

_____ My Score

15 Top Score

Extension
Write six sentences with words studied in this lesson.

43

Lesson 36

Verb Forms: *Knew/Known, Grew/Grown, Flew/Flown, Threw/Thrown, Blew/Blown, Drew/Drawn*

Rule	Example
Use *knew, grew, flew, threw, blew,* and *drew* alone.	The wind **blew** hard.
Use *known, grown, flown, thrown, blown,* and *drawn* with a helping verb such as *is, am, are, was, were, has, have,* or *had.*	The cup **was blown** across the road.

Circle the correct word.

1. The Alvarez family **knew known** the way to the fair in Seattle.

2. Mrs. Alvarez had **draw drawn** the route on a map.

3. Fina **grew grown** restless as the car trip **drawn drew** to an end.

4. Traffic **grew grown** very heavy near the fair entrance.

5. The wind **blew blown** a paper cup that someone had **threw thrown** from a car window.

6. Luis **knew known** that the person **knew known** not to litter.

7. "Someone **threw thrown** that cup from the car ahead of us," said Luis.

8. Fina **grew grown** annoyed.

9. "Littering has **grew grown** to be a big problem," she said.

10. Mr. Alvarez **knew known** of one litterer who had been fined $500.

11. The discussion **grew grown** lively.

12. Before they **knew known** it, the Alvarez family had arrived at the fair.

Count 1 point for each correct answer.

_____ **My Score**

15 Top Score

Extension
Write a letter to a friend about something that recently happened to you. Use some words learned in this lesson.

Name _____

Review Lessons 31–36

● **Revise these sentences to correct the dangling participles.**

1. Running to catch the bus, the groceries dropped in the street.

   _____

2. Walking into the doctor's office, the skeleton surprised me.

   _____

3. Filled with sand, the children played a fast game of Hackysack.

   _____

● **Circle the correct word.**

4. Pam had **rang rung** the doorbell.

5. Some guests have **ate eaten** more than two sandwiches.

6. They have never **swam swum** just after eating.

7. What have they **gone went** to see?

8. What kind of exhibit **came come** to the museum?

9. We have **did done** a smart thing.

10. Our lawn mower is **broke broken.**

11. What have you **written wrote?**

12. We **began begin** to slow down.

13. Frost had **froze frozen** on the man's beard.

14. We had **grew grown** restless at the movie.

15. We should have **flew flown** to Omaha.

Count 1 point for
each correct answer.

_____ My Score
15 Top Score

UNIT 2: Usage

45

Lesson 37

Negatives

Rule	Example
Use **isn't**, **wasn't**, and **doesn't** when you talk about one and with the word **it**.	**Isn't** Paul's computer new? He **doesn't** know how to program it well yet.
Use **aren't**, **weren't**, and **don't** when you talk about more than one and with the word **you**.	**Aren't** Paul's friends eager to use it? **Weren't** you there?
Use **wasn't** and **don't** with the word **I**.	I **wasn't** with them.

Circle the correct word.

1. **Aren't Isn't** it true that the economy is the most important issue facing the country?

2. **Doesn't Don't** you believe you need to know how our economy works?

3. **Aren't Isn't** customs, rights, and responsibilities things that all Americans share?

4. **Wasn't Weren't** that part of our Declaration of Independence?

5. Our forefathers **aren't weren't** only concerned about those things but also about trading with other countries.

6. **Aren't Isn't** profit the money a business earns after it pays for its costs?

7. **Aren't Isn't** looking for the job we want part of our economy too?

8. Most people today **aren't isn't** involved in farming as much as they were in the past.

9. I **doesn't don't** know what job I'll have in the future.

10. We **aren't isn't** limited in what we can dream.

Count 1 point for each correct answer.

_____ My Score

10 Top Score

Extension
Write a paragraph about a time you *weren't* lucky.

Lesson 38

Double Negatives

Rule	Example
Words like **no, never, not, no one, none, scarcely,** and **hardly** are called **negatives.** Only one negative should be used in expressing an idea.	Correct: Dan has **no** pet. Incorrect: Dan **hasn't no** pet.
Not is written **n't** in contractions. Do not use another negative with a contraction ending in **n't.**	Correct: Dan **hasn't** a pet. Incorrect: Dan **hasn't no** pet.

Circle the correct word.

1. There aren't   **any   none**   of my friends who have seen the movie *Titanic*.

2. Aren't   **any   no**   theaters showing it in our town?

3. I haven't   **ever   never**   seen it either.

4. The ship didn't have   **none   some**   of the rescue equipment that ships do today.

5. About 700 people   **could   couldn't**   scarcely get on the lifeboats.

6. There wasn't   **any   no**   ship close enough to rescue   **any   no**   other survivors in time.

7. There wasn't   **anything   nothing**   else that could be done for them.

8. They couldn't go   **anywhere   nowhere**   for help.

9. There hasn't been   **any   no**   worse ship disaster in history.

10. When the wreck was found in 1985, weren't there   **no   some**   pictures taken?

11. Haven't you   **ever   never**   seen them?

12. They didn't recover   **any   no**   artifacts until 1987.

13. Didn't they include   **no   some**   dishes, jewels, and coins?

14. Scientists believe that the damage wasn't to   **no   some**   large area, but to a crucial area of the ship.

Count 1 point for each correct answer.

_____ My Score

15 Top Score

Extension
Tell your classmates about a pet you have or would like to have.

Lesson 39

Verbs: *Lie/Lay, Sit/Set*

Rule	Example
The verb **lie** means to rest or recline. Its forms are **lie, lies, lying, lay,** and **lain.**	May I **lie** here to rest? Silver **lay** there yesterday. He **has lain** there often.
The verb **lay** means to place or put an object somewhere. Its forms are **lay, lays, laying,** and **laid.**	**Lay** your books on the table. I **laid** the pictures there.
The verb **sit** means to rest or to have a seat. Its forms are **sits, sitting,** and **sat.**	She **was sitting** there before I **sat** down here.
The verb **set** means to put or place something. Other forms of the verb **set** are **sets** and **setting.**	Jenny **set** the boxes in the car. Mr. Reed **is setting** the tent near the lake.

Write the correct form of *lay* or *lie* to complete each sentence.

1. My dog Bailey likes to _____ in the sun during the day.

2. Where has he _____ at night?

3. Will Thomas _____ on the bed after he _____ the kittens in the box?

4. Where has he _____ the tails of the kites?

Use a form of *sit* or *set* to complete each sentence.

5. Don't just _____ there if you hear the fire alarm.

6. After she had _____ a few minutes longer, Jenny _____ the boxes in the Jeep.

7. José is _____ under the tree where I _____ the tent.

Count 1 point for each correct answer.

_____ My Score

10 Top Score

Extension
Write four sentences: one each using one of the forms of *lie, lay, sit,* and *set.*

Lesson 40

Verbs: May/Can, Bring/Take

Rule	Example
Use **may** to ask or give permission. Use **can** to show ability to do something.	**May** we eat the cookies now? You **may** eat them if you **can** wait 10 more minutes.
Bring means to carry from a far place to a nearer place. **Take** means to carry from a nearby place to a place farther away.	I will **bring** the rake when I come. **Take** the shovel with you.

Circle the correct word.

1. **Can May** I tell you about my new sport—archery?

2. I **can may** talk about it for hours.

3. **Bring Take** me that book, and I'll show you what a quiver is.

4. **Can May** you see this famous picture of William Tell?

5. I **can may bring take** in my gloves from the car and show you how they are worn.

6. I **bring take** a bracer to my lessons at the archery center to protect my arm from the bowstring.

7. I **can may** tell the difference between a crossbow and a longbow.

8. A footbow, in which the arrow is drawn back with both hands, **can may** shoot an arrow well over a mile.

9. **Can May** you **bring take** me those targets over there so I **can may** show you the bull's-eye?

10. I'll have to **bring take** you to the archery center to show you around.

11. We **can may** bring visitors on Saturdays.

12. **Can may** you go at noon?

Count 1 point for each correct answer.

_____ My Score
15 Top Score

Extension
Write four sentences, one with each of the four words studied in this lesson.

Adjectives and Adverbs: Choosing an Adjective or an Adverb

Rule	Example
An **adjective** is a word used to modify a noun or a pronoun. It tells what kind, which one, how many, or how much.	They are **careful** riders.
An **adverb** is a word used to modify a verb, an adjective, or another adverb. Adverbs tell when, where, how, and to what degree.	They ride their bicycles **carefully**.

On the line before each sentence, write _adj_ if the word in bold type is an adjective or _adv_ if it is an adverb.

1. _____ Louisa May Alcott wrote _Little Women_ in an **attractive** house in Concord, Massachusetts.

2. _____ Some old houses fall apart **badly.**

3. _____ But the Alcotts' home is in **good** shape.

4. _____ The guide **there** said that many possessions of the Alcotts were preserved.

5. _____ Alcott's room has the **semicircular** desk where she wrote _Little Women._

6. _____ She **always** wrote in a graceful hand.

7. _____ The novel was an **instant** success.

8. _____ It is about Alcott's own **happy** home life.

9. _____ The dining room was the stage for their dramas in which Alcott **always** preferred the part of a boy.

10. _____ Then the girls would race **quickly** up the stairs to change costumes.

Count 1 point for each correct answer.

_____ My Score

10 Top Score

Extension
Write four sentences, one each using _good, well, bad,_ and _badly._

50

Lesson 42

Using Prepositions

Rule	Example
Use **into** to mean from the outside to the inside. Use **in** to mean within a place.	The Blakes moved **into** their house in December. They have lived **in** the house for a year.
Use **to** when suggesting motion from one place to another. Use **at** when telling where a person or thing is.	Pam will go **to** the Blakes' home. Tim is **at** home.
Use **between** when you speak of two persons or things. Use **among** when you speak of more than two persons or things.	Carol had to choose **between** an apple and a banana. The house is located **among** the trees.

Circle the correct word.

1. Soon after the United States gained its independence, there was conflict **among between** the states.

2. In 1787, delegates traveled **at to** Philadelphia to discuss the new nation.

3. They came **in into** the meeting hall ready with their speeches.

4. **In Into** Philadelphia, the delegates passed the Articles of Confederation.

5. One law let people move **in into** the Northwest Territory.

6. There was disagreement **among between** two groups about slavery.

7. A compromise was finally reached **among between** the 55 delegates.

8. They stayed **at to** Philadelphia until September.

9. Afterwards, the delegates returned **at to** their home states.

10. You can see the Liberty Bell **in into** Philadelphia.

Extension
Tell your classmates about a time you had to choose between two things.

Count 1 point for each correct answer.

_____ My Score
10 Top Score

51

Review Lessons 37–42

- **Circle the correct word.**

1. Jorge hasn't **ever   never**   had a pet.

2. There isn't **any   no**   room in his family's apartment for one.

3. The rules of the apartment house don't allow **any   no**   pets.

4. My dog is supposed to **lay   lie**   on his rug.

5. He **lay   lie**   in front of the fireplace yesterday.

6. Tomas **lay   laid**   the books on his desk.

7. "I am **laying   lying**   them here for just a moment," he said.

8. Mrs. Reed is **setting   sitting**   a pile of blankets on a chair.

9. We **sat   set**   at the first table at the wedding.

10. You **can   may**   carry the tools if you think you **can   may.**

11. We **can   may**   go home after you **bring   take**   out the trash.

12. We went **in   into**   the game room at our grandparents' home.

13. **Among   Between**   the five cousins, we decided on a game.

14. When everyone was seated **at   to**   the table, the game began.

- **On the line before each sentence, write *adj* if the word in bold type is an adjective or *adv* if it is an adverb.**

15. _____ We had a **good** day.

16. _____ We played **well.**

17. _____ Saturday was a **bright** sunny day.

18. _____ The sun shone **brightly.**

Count 1 point for
each correct answer.

_____ My Score
20 Top Score

UNIT 2: Usage

Cumulative Review
Units 1–2

•Unit 1   **Underline the common nouns and circle the proper nouns.**

1. Cleopatra was the 21-year-old ruler of Egypt.

2. Julius Caesar helped Cleopatra defeat her brother.

3. She gave Julius Caesar money he needed to fight for control of Rome.

4. He returned in triumph to Rome and made himself dictator.

•Unit 1   **Write the possessive form of the word in parentheses.**

5. 1998 was one of _____ most exciting seasons in years. (baseball)

6. Mark _____ 70 home runs set a new record. (McGwire)

•Unit 1   **Circle each pronoun.**

7. My family visited Florida last May.

8. We drove to the Kennedy Space Center in our new van.

9. Our next trip is to Mount Rushmore.

•Unit 1   **Circle the indirect object.**

10. The teacher showed us the way to make pizza.

11. He told you how long to let the dough rise.

•Unit 1   **Above each word write the word's part of speech. Use *n* for *noun*, *v* for *verb*, *pron* for *pronoun*, *adj* for *adjective*, *adv* for *adverb*, *prep* for *preposition*, *conj* for *conjunction*, and *i* for *interjection*.**

12. For 2,000 years, scientists have classified groups of living things.

13. One early system grouped all living things as plants or animals.

•Unit 2   **Write the contractions of these words.**

14. he will _____   17. she would _____

15. let us _____   18. it will _____

16. it has _____   19. does not _____

Cumulative Review

•Unit 2   **Circle the correct word.**

20. **Who's Whose** Gandhi?

21. I think **you're your** studying him in history class.

22. **Theirs There's** a section in our book about him.

23. **It's Its** in the section on world events.

•Unit 2   **Write the correct form of the verb in parentheses.**

24. *Lincoln at Gettysburg* was _____ by Garry Wills. (write)

25. The wasps _____ me four times. (sting)

•Unit 2   **Circle the correct word.**

26. Thomas Edison **was were** the inventor of the lightbulb.

27. The electric generating system and the movie projector **are is** some of the inventions that shaped the twentieth century.

•Unit 2   **Revise this sentence to correct the dangling participle.**

28. Lost in the airport, it was difficult to understand the signs.

_____

•Unit 2   **On the line before each sentence, write *adj* if the word in bold type is an adjective or *adv* if it is an adverb.**

29. _____ The dog's **thoughtless** owner let it run loose.

30. _____ It was barking **loudly.**

31. _____ The dog **happily** licked John's hand.

Count 1 point for each correct answer.

_____ **My Score**
60 Top Score

UNIT 2 Inventory

Write the contractions of these words.   Lesson 19

1. you will _____

2. that is _____

3. do not _____

4. should not _____

5. you are _____

6. they will _____

Circle the correct word.   Lesson 22

7. I know **you're your** on the soccer team.

8. **Who's Whose** the coach?

9. The team plays **it's its** first game tonight.

Cross out the pronouns that are not needed.   Lesson 24

10. Some people they think that the Beatles they were the most influential band of the rock music era.

11. Beatlemania it hit the U.S. when the Beatles appeared on the *Ed Sullivan Show* in the 1960s.

12. Ed Sullivan he had a very popular variety show.

Write the correct form of the verb in parentheses.   Lesson 27

13. We _____ 3 miles in track yesterday. (run)

14. Explorers _____ gold in the New World. (seek)

Circle the correct word.   Lesson 28

15. The computer **had has** transformed industry and society.

16. Bill Gates **are is** a pioneer in personal computer operating systems.

Revise this sentence to correct the dangling participle.   Lesson 31

17. Climbing to the top of the hill, the Capitol could be seen.

_____

Circle the correct word.   Lesson 32–36

18. I **lend lent** Mom a dollar yesterday.

19. Amelia **fling flung** the toy out of the crib.

20. Have you **bought buy** the gift?

Circle the correct word.   Lessons 39–40

21. We **can can't** scarcely lift this table.

22. Couldn't **any no** other people help us?

23. Dad likes to **lay lie** in his hammock.

24. **Can May** I **bring take** this snack to school?

Circle the correct word.   Lesson 42

25. We walked **among between** the flowers, then **among between** two trees.

26. Then we went **in into** the house for dinner.

27. We sat **at to** the table.

Count 1 point for each correct answer.

_____ My Score

30 Top Score

Lesson 43

Capitalization: Proper Nouns

Rule	Example
Capitalize **proper nouns**. A proper noun names a **particular** person, place, thing, or idea.	My little brother likes **McDonalds**. Have you ever seen the **Statue of Liberty?**

Circle each letter that should be a capital.

1. The henry ford museum in dearborn, michigan, is a fascinating place to visit.

2. The first shots of the american revolution were fired at the battle of lexington.

3. Like earth's moon, mercury is covered with craters.

4. The golden gate bridge is in san francisco, california.

5. The empire state building is 102 stories high.

6. My aunt was a nurse during world war II.

7. president Ulysses S. Grant was a commander of union forces during the civil war.

8. The red cross was founded by Clara Barton.

9. President Harding was a member of the united states senate.

10. He was a member of the republican party from ohio.

11. Michael Jordan helped the chicago bulls win six NBA championships.

12. My sister's little league team is named the mustangs.

13. I think I bought my bike at sears.

Extension
Write a paragraph about an issue you would like to see addressed by Congress.

Count 1 point for each correct answer.

_____ My Score
40 Top Score

Lesson 44

Capitalization: The Word I, Names, Days, Months, Holidays

Rule	Example
Always write the word **I** as a capital letter.	Jose and **I** are good friends.
Use a capital letter to begin each word in a **person's name.**	Our 16th president was **Abraham Lincoln.**
Capitalize words that refer to relatives when used as a name or with a name.	Has **Uncle Quinn** called? I believe that **Mother** spoke to him.
Do not capitalize words that refer to relatives after the words **my, our, his, her,** or **their.**	Lydia is **my uncle's sister.**
Always begin the name of a **month,** a **day of the week,** and a **holiday** with a capital letter. All main words in the name of a holiday begin with a capital letter.	The **Fourth of July** is an important day in our country's history. We often refer to it as **Independence Day.**
The names of the seasons begin with lowercase letters.	The four seasons are **winter, spring, summer,** and **fall.**

Circle each letter that should be a capital.

1. Last july i went to Washington, D.C., for independence day.

2. My mother and uncle john came too.

3. This friday mother and i are going back to Washington.

4. We'll visit uncle John next summer.

Count 1 point for each correct answer.

_____ My Score

10 Top Score

Extension
Write a paragraph about your favorite holiday and how you celebrate it.

Lesson 45

Capitalization and Punctuation: Titles of People and Abbreviations

Rule	Example
A title such as **General** or **President** should begin with a capital letter when it is used with the name of a person.	Did you know that **President Lincoln** was born in Kentucky?
Abbreviations, such as the titles **Mr.**, **Mrs.**, and **Ms.**, should be followed by a period.	The company sent the brochures to **Mr. and Mrs. Chin.**
Initials are followed by a period. If initials are at the end of a sentence, do not add a sentence period.	My middle initial is **S.**

Circle every letter that should be a capital. Place periods where needed.

1. My brother had a meeting with dean Anders on his first day of college.

2. I believe sen Wilford can see you now.

3. Is lt Ward here yet?

4. Are mr and mrs Bennett related to you?

5. Franklin d Roosevelt was our longest-serving president.

6. My brother goes by the name am Walton.

7. Elizabeth's initials are era

8. In 1960, John f Kennedy ran for the presidency.

9. We had an award for principal Martinez and nurse Arnold.

10. We celebrate the birthday of Martin Luther King jr in January.

11. Did rep C Canton vote for the bill?

Extension
Look through the newspaper and share with the class some abbreviations you find.

Count 1 point for each correct answer.

_____ My Score
30 Top Score

Lesson 46

UNIT 3: Mechanics

Capitalization: Place Names, Organizations, Nationalities

Rule	Example
Capitalize place names, the name of a building or memorial, the name of a street or highway, and the name of a club or organization.	Yellowstone National Park U. S. Highway 81 Boy Scouts of America
Capitalize the name of a country or a nationality and a word made from the name of a country or a nationality.	We met several **Japanese** tourists on our visit to **Spain.**

Circle each letter that should be a capital.

1. new york is one of the largest cities in the united states.

2. tokyo, japan; shanghai, china; and mexico city, mexico, are also among the world's largest cities.

3. Mr. and Mrs. Wells went to new york city.

4. On Monday, October 1, they arrived at kennedy airport.

5. They spent the afternoon walking on fifth avenue.

6. Their friend has a poodle that she often walks in central park.

7. She is a member of the girl scouts of america.

8. Then they saw a native american exhibit at the metropolitan museum of art.

9. Last night they saw a ballet at lincoln center.

10. Tonight they plan to visit chinatown and enjoy a chinese dinner.

11. Tomorrow they may have italian or french food.

12. When they return to boise, Idaho, they will be ready for a rest!

Count 1 point for each correct answer.

_____ My Score

35 Top Score

Extension
Research and write a report on the people of any country you wish.

Lesson 47

Capitalization and Punctuation: Titles

Rule	Example
Begin the first word and every important word with a capital letter in the title of a **book**, a **movie**, a **play**, or a **magazine**.	I have seen *Romeo and Juliet* four times.
When you write about a book, movie, play, or painting, **underline** the title of the book. Make the title **italic** when you are using a computer.	*Our class is reading the book S.O.R. Losers.* Our class is reading the book *S.O.R. Losers.*
Enclose the title of a story, a poem, or a song with **quotation marks** when it is used in a sentence.	Father's favorite song is **"Home on the Range."** Our principal read us the story **"Felicity Goes Home."**

Circle each letter that should be a capital and insert punctuation.

1. Miss Fuller asked Daryl whether he had read the poem johnny appleseed.

2. Daryl said he had not read it but that he had read the poem the road not taken.

3. "There are several poems in each issue of children's digest," Maria said.

4. "Have you read the book house of the four winds?" Armando asked.

5. Maria said one of her favorite stories is the firebird, which she found in a book called old peter's russian tales by Arthur Ransome.

6. She asked whether anyone had seen the play the pirates of penzance.

7. Diana said she had seen it but preferred the play brigadoon.

8. Diana said the best poem in that book is called the laughing time.

9. My favorite patriotic song is the star-spangled banner.

10. Have you seen the movie forrest gump with Tom Hanks?

Count 1 point for each correct answer.

_____ **My Score**

45 Top Score

Extension
Make a list of the movies you have seen and books you have read recently. Use proper punctuation.

Lesson 48

Punctuation: Semicolons

Rule	Example
Use a semicolon between **two sentences** joined by words such as *therefore, in fact, however, for example,* and *nevertheless.*	Our car was broken; therefore, we had to find another ride.
Use a semicolon to separate the items in a **series** when the items contain commas.	My schedule is Period 1, English; Period 2, Math; and Period 3, History.

Insert semicolons where needed.

1. Holiday traffic has always been a danger to safety for example, hundreds were killed last year.

2. The problem of tardies is growing in fact, it will be addressed soon by the faculty.

3. Tension rose during the meeting nevertheless, most of the city council members remained calm.

4. Matters involving our district's schools were discussed therefore, representatives were invited to attend.

5. The foreign situation was getting worse however, all governments remained optimistic.

6. My sisters and their birthdays are Tonda, July 7 Deidra, May 31 and Janelle, October 24.

7. The tour group went to Paris, France Salzburg, Austria Florence, Italy and London, England.

8. The people who influenced my choice of college were Ms. Mason, my German teacher Mr. Osborn, my guidance counselor and Ms. Miller, my employer.

9. The officers elected are Sandra, president Audrey, vice-president Ashley, secretary and Jenna, treasurer.

Count 1 point for each correct answer.

_____ **My Score**

15 Top Score

Extension
Write a sentence listing five states and their capitals.

Review Lessons 43–48

- **Circle every letter that should be a capital. Place periods where needed.**

1. What do you do on thanksgiving day?

2. We always gather at aunt Ellen's house.

3. Thanksgiving is celebrated on the fourth thursday in november.

4. It was first observed by the pilgrims in 1621.

5. My grandfather is a member of the seattle sailing and rowing club.

6. She has danish, norwegian, and french ancestors.

7. I think i would like to join the federal bureau of investigation.

8. Mother's initials are nmw

9. The sears tower is the tallest building in the United States.

10. Our neighbor's name is jane walsh.

11. She is also known as sen walsh.

- **Circle each letter that should be a capital and insert the needed punctuation marks.**

12. Jack has been reading the book island of the blue dolphins.

13. A good play is oklahoma.

14. If you like poems, you should read alabaster annie.

15. Amanda gets american girls magazine.

- **Insert semicolons where needed.**

16. There were several reasons for the Civil War for example, the North and the South disagreed over slavery.

17. I have already eaten however, I will join you for dessert.

Count 1 point for each correct answer.

_____ **My Score**
45 Top Score

Punctuation: Commas in Series, Dates, and Places

Rule	Example
Use a comma to separate words in a **series.**	Randy, Peg, and Bill came to our party.
Use a comma to separate the name of a **city** from its **state or country** and the state or country from the rest of the sentence.	We drove to Chicago, Illinois, last month.
Use a comma to separate the name of a **day** from the name of a **month**; the **day** of the month from the **year**; and the **year** from the rest of the sentence.	My sister was born on Friday, August 6, 1999, in Tampa.

Insert the needed commas.

1. An hour on Friday November 10 was set aside to study poetry.

2. What a kind gentle and sympathetic person Longfellow must have been.

3. He was born on February 27 1807 in Maine.

4. Wasn't he a teacher as well as a poet novelist and scholar?

5. He taught at Bowdoin College in Brunswick Maine before going to Harvard.

6. "Evangeline" "The Song of Hiawatha" and "The Courtship of Miles Standish" brought him fame in his own time.

7. We studied poems by Emily Dickinson that included "I Died for Beauty" "The Bustle in the House" and "A Light Exists in Spring."

8. Emily Dickinson was born on December 10 1830 in Amherst Massachusetts and is remembered for poems about beauty love and nature.

Count 1 point for each correct answer.

_____ **My Score**
20 Top Score

Extension
Write a sentence listing three of your favorite books. Proofread for correct comma use.

Lesson 50   UNIT 3: Mechanics

Punctuation: Commas with Direct Address and Introductory Words and Phrases

Rule	Example
Use a comma to set off words or names in **direct address**.	Nate, are you ready for the test? I can get you some water, sir, if you like.
Use a comma to set off **yes, no,** or **please.**	Yes, you may sit there. Please, get ready for lunch. Get ready, please, for lunch.
Use a comma after **introductory words and phrases.**	In order to finish the project by Tuesday, you need to start today. In December, my family visits Grandma.

Insert commas where needed.

1. I don't know Alice what language is spoken in Algeria.

2. Please Ben try researching that topic on the Internet.

3. When you find out let me know.

4. In Trinidad and Tobago English is spoken.

5. Emil find out please what language is spoken in Sweden.

6. While in Benin try the French you learned in school.

7. In order to communicate in Brazil it would be helpful to speak Portuguese.

8. David can you find Burundi on the globe?

9. No I have never been there.

10. Your report is excellent Samantha.

11. Yes you got an A.

Count 1 point for
each correct answer.   _____ **My Score**
                                   15 Top Score

Extension
Write three sentences using commas as learned
in this lesson.

64

Punctuation and Capitalization: Letters

A **business letter** is a letter you write to a person at a company. Besides what you write (the body), there are four main parts of a business letter.

Rule	Example
The **heading** is your address and the date.	300 North Central San Diego, CA 92041 October 1, 2001
The **inside address** includes the person and company to which you are writing. Put a comma between the city and the state.	Mr. Gerald Smith Newberry Industries 4950 Main Street Lancaster, OH 17601
Begin the **greeting** with a capital letter. Put a colon at the end of the greeting. Capitalize the first word of the **closing.** Put a comma at the end of the closing.	Dear Mr. Smith: Sincerely,

Circle each letter that should be a capital. Put punctuation where needed. Draw a line through one letter that should be lowercase.

636 East Welden Street

Denver CO 80202

July 5 2001

Ms. Inez Bradley

Columbia City Hall

569 Center Circle

Columbia MD 12756

dear Ms. Bradley

    thank you so much for coming to our class last week and telling us about your job as a judge. Maybe we could come visit you at City Hall

yours Truly

Count 1 point for each correct answer.   _____ My Score
10 Top Score

Extension
Write a business letter to a company explaining what you like about a product it makes.

Lesson **52**

Punctuation: Coordinating Conjunctions and Subordinate Clauses

Rule	Example
Two related sentences may be connected by a **coordinating conjunction.** Place a comma before the coordinating conjunction.	I like football. She likes basketball. I like football, **and** she likes basketball.
A **subordinate clause** has a subject and a predicate but does not express a complete thought, so it cannot stand alone as a sentence. Put a **comma** after the subordinate clause.	**While you are in Philadelphia**, see the Liberty Bell.

Some words that begin a subordinate clause are **as, because, before, if, unless, when, where,** and **whether.**

Combine these sentences. Draw an arrow where the coordinating conjunction in parentheses should go. Correct punctuation as necessary. Circle the letters that should be lowercase.

1. Mary McLeod Bethune opened her school for girls in 1904. She had 250 students within two years. (and)

2. The school grew. In 1923, it merged with Cookman Institute. (and)

3. Bethune later became the president of a college. She still remembered her "childish dreams in the cotton fields." (but)

Circle the subordinate clause.

4. While Bethune lived in Daytona Beach, she expanded her civil rights work.

Count 1 point for each correct answer.

_____ My Score
10 Top Score

Extension
Write one sentence with a coordinating conjunction and one sentence with a subordinate clause.

Lesson 53

Punctuation: Commas with Appositives

Rule	Example
An **appositive** is a word or phrase that identifies or gives more information about a noun. Use a comma to set off an appositive.	We like to eat at Saska, **a restaurant near our home.** "A restaurant near our home" identifies "Saska." Her car, **a silver sedan,** is parked outside. "A silver sedan" identifies "car."

Circle each appositive. Underline the noun that is identified or explained by the appositive.

1. Wave Rock, near Hyden, Australia, is a spectacular formation.

2. Scientists estimate that the rock, a wave-shaped structure, is very old.

3. Its size, 15 meters high and several hundred meters long, makes it a fabulous rock to study.

4. Rocks, looking hard and unchanging, are actually constantly being changed by the forces of nature.

5. Rocks are broken down by wind, one of the weathering forces of nature.

Extension
Write a sentence with an appositive.

Count 1 point for each correct answer.

_____ My Score
10 Top Score

Lesson 54

Punctuation: Direct Quotations

The exact words said by someone are called a **direct quotation.**

Rule	Example
Capitalize the first word of a direct quotation. Enclose the words of a direct quotation in quotation marks. Separate the quotation from the person saying it with a comma.	"I read that book for class," Fiona said.
When a sentence being quoted has words in the middle of it, separate the two parts with commas and add another set of quotation marks. Always place the comma inside the quotation mark. Do not capitalize the first word of the second part unless it is a proper noun.	"Don't buy a book," Dan said, "because I can loan you one."
If the quoted sentence ends with a question mark or an exclamation point, do not add a comma.	"How are you doing on your report?" asked Ms. Anderson.

Circle each letter that should be a capital. Put in the needed quotation marks and commas.

1. that's one small step for man, one giant leap for mankind declared Neil Armstrong as he set foot on the moon in 1969.

2. John F. Kennedy said ask not what your country can do for you; ask what you can do for your country.

3. whatever you do said David Rockefeller, if you do it hard enough, you'll enjoy it.

4. genius is one percent inspiration said Thomas Edison, and ninety-nine percent perspiration.

Extension
Find a famous quote and write it on a piece of paper. Proofread for correct punctuation.

Count 1 point for each correct answer. _____ **My Score** 20 Top Score

68

Review Lessons 49–54

- **Insert commas where needed.**

1. Steel copper cattle and hay are some important products of Utah.

2. Arizona became a state on February 14 1912 and is known as the Grand Canyon State.

3. Please Alicia show us the Baltic Sea on the globe.

4. In order to understand atoms it might be helpful to look at this model.

- **Circle each letter that should be a capital. Put punctuation where needed.**

5353 Waddell Road   dear Mr. Karl
Chattanooga TN 37401
September 2 2001   yours truly

- **Circle the subordinate clause and add the comma.**

5. As I was heading into the classroom I slipped on some water.

- **Circle each appositive and underline the noun that is identified or explained by the appositive.**

6. William Henry Harrison, our ninth president, served only 31 days.

- **Circle each letter that should be a capital. Put in the needed quotation marks and commas.**

7. hindsight is always twenty-twenty said film director Billy Wilder.

8. Put your pencils down said our teacher.

Count 1 point for each correct answer.

_____ **My Score**
25 Top Score

Cumulative Review   Units 1–3

•Unit 1   **Write the correct form of the verb in parentheses after the sentence.**

1. Ricky Williams _____ the Heisman Trophy in 1998. (win)

2. Valery Ivanovich Tokarev _____ on the *Discovery* mission to space in 1999. (is)

•Unit 1   **Circle the indirect object.**

3. Throw me the ball.

4. I will send him my bill tomorrow.

5. Tom gave Shannon a puppy.

•Unit 1   **Circle the nouns and underline the adjectives.**

6. The space shuttle named *Atlantis* docked with the space station named *Mir* for the first time in history.

•Unit 2   **Write the contractions of these words.**

7. cannot _____   9. he is _____

8. we will _____   10. are not _____

•Unit 2   **Circle the correct word.**

11. **You're Your** a great volleyball player.

12. **Who's Whose** going to win the World Series?

13. The weatherperson said **it's its** going to be a cold winter.

14. The team **are is** ahead right now.

15. We **could couldn't** hardly believe the story, but **it's   its**   true.

16. Maggie is sitting **in into** her room.

17. Choose **among between** these two pieces of cake.

18. The group had **driven drove** a long way the first day.

19. I'm sure I **laid lay** my wallet there.

Cumulative Review

•Unit 3   **Circle each letter that should be a capital. Place periods where needed.**

20.   boxing day is celebrated in australia, canada, great britain, and new zealand.

21.   Did i tell you that aunt Sue and uncle Tim called from the chinese restaurant?

22.   Are your initials ami?

•Unit 3   **Insert commas where needed.**

23.   John Adams Thomas Jefferson and Theodore Roosevelt were all vice-presidents of the United States before becoming presidents.

24.   Iowa became a state on December 28 1846 and is known as the Hawkeye State.

•Unit 3   **Circle each letter that should be a capital. Put punctuation where needed.**

103 North Willow Avenue   Ms. Season Minot   dear Ms. Minot

Waterloo IL 62298   ARE Company

May 12 2001   2421 Grove Street

                          Galveston TX 77550   yours truly

•Unit 3   **Combine these sentences. Draw an arrow where the coordinating conjunction in parentheses should go. Correct punctuation as needed**

25.   Tennessee became a state on June 1, 1796. Kentucky became a state on June 1, 1792. (and)

Count 1 point for each correct answer.   _____ My Score

                                                65 Top Score

UNIT 3 Inventory

Circle each letter that should be a capital. Place periods where needed.

Lessons 43–46

1. My family was in canada for canada day, which is july 1.

2. I always enjoy visiting aunt Sunee and uncle Chet in thailand.

3. My spanish class celebrated mexican independence day on september 16.

4. Yes, i can introduce you to united states rep janet carr.

5. Her initials are jec

Insert semicolons where needed.

Lesson 48

6. Some holidays and their countries are Carnival, Brazil Constitution Day, Norway and Bastille Day, France.

Insert commas where needed.

Lessons 49, 50

7. Precipitation is water that falls to Earth as rain snow hail or sleet.

8. Nine hospitals three universities and three colleges are located in Mobile Alabama.

9. In the South China Sea many islands make up the country of Indonesia.

10. No Martin we can't go there for a field trip.

11. Yes we may be able to go to the zoo.

12. Because of the monsoon Arizona gets rain in August.

Circle each letter that should be a capital. Put punctuation where needed.

Lesson 51

72 Redwood Street

Baton Rouge LA 70821

March 18 2001

Ms. Paula Quincy

K.F.J. Corporation

48 Boston Avenue

Cambridge MA 02139

Dear Ms. Quincy

yours truly

Circle the subordinate clause and add the comma.

Lesson 52

13. Because I majored in Spanish I was able to live in Spain my senior year.

Circle each appositive and underline the noun that is identified or explained by the appositive.

Lesson 53

14. A hurricane, called a typhoon in the Pacific Ocean, is a violent storm that develops at sea.

15. I enjoy boating, a great way to relax on a sunny day.

Count 1 point for each correct answer.

_____ **My Score**

50 Top Score

Lesson 55

Context Clues

> You can sometimes figure out the meaning of the word from its **context,** the words and sentences around it. Writers give **context clues** in five main ways.
>
> **Definition** The meaning of the word is stated.
>
> **Example** The meaning of the unfamiliar word is explained through examples.
>
> **Comparison** The unfamiliar word is similar to a familiar word or phrase.
>
> **Contrast** The unfamiliar word is opposite a familiar word or phrase.
>
> **Cause and Effect** The unfamiliar word is explained as part of a cause-and-effect relationship.

Match the type of context clue with the sentence in which it is used. Write the meaning of the bold word.

a. definition   b. example   c. comparison   d. contrast   e. cause and effect

1. _____ There are few theaters here, but on Broadway, there are

   theaters **galore.** _____

2. _____ She is such a **malapert.** I've never seen anyone so sassy. _____

3. _____ I am taking **anthropology,** which is the study of human beings.

   _____

4. _____ **Junk art**—art made from discarded materials, for example—is popular

   in our neighborhood. _____

5. _____ I know I looked **perplexed,** because his arguments always leave

   me puzzled. _____

Count 1 point for
each correct answer.

_____ My Score
10 Top Score

Extension
Write a short paragraph giving context clues for
a bold word. Have a partner figure out the
meaning of the word.

Lesson 56   UNIT 4: Vocabulary

Synonyms and Antonyms

Rule	Example
Words that mean the same or nearly the same are called **synonyms**.	I have already **started** to work. Why don't you **begin**?
Words that are opposite in meaning are called **antonyms**.	I **forgot** my umbrella, but I **remembered** to wear my raincoat.

answer	illustration	weary	slowly	tame
funny	oral	enemies	soft	worse

Write a synonym for the word or words in parentheses. Use words from the list above.

1. We are waiting for an _____ to the letter we sent them. (reply)

2. Ten _____ campers trooped into camp after a long hike. (tired)

3. _____ language is often less exact than written language. (spoken)

4. Everyone thought the clowns were very _____. (comical)

5. The teacher asked us to use at least one _____ in each report. (example, picture, drawing)

Write an antonym for the word in bold type. Use words from the list above.

6. Dogs were **wild** animals many years ago, but they are now _____ animals.

7. Dogs and cats are **friends** to people but _____ to rats and mice.

8. Reynaldo's grade on the test was **better** than Hector's but _____ than Mae's.

9. A paved road stays **hard** in a rainstorm, but a dirt road becomes _____.

10. A swallow flies **swiftly,** but a crow flies _____.

Count 1 point for each correct answer.

_____ **My Score**
10 Top Score

Extension
Make a list of five words and their synonyms and five words and their antonyms.

Lesson 57

Homophones

> ### Rule
> Words that are pronounced alike but have different meanings and different spellings are called **homophones**.
>
> ### Example
> **Our** show will start in an **hour**.

Circle the correct word.

1. Juan and Maria were putting on **their there they're** coats at **one won** o'clock.

2. "Hurry," said Scott. "We have **to too two** get **their there they're** before the show starts **sew so** we can **buy by bye** tickets."

3. "**Wait Weight** a minute. I can't **find fined** my hat," said Juan.

4. Maria said, "**Hear Here** it is. **You're Your** hat should **knot not** have **been bin in inn** my room."

5. Juan had left his **read red** hat there **to too two** dry after he was caught in the **rain reign rein.**

6. When they arrived, **know no one won** was **in inn** the box office. They saw a sign that **read red** "Sold Out."

7. "I **told tolled ewe you** we should have left earlier," said Scott. "Now we can't **buy by bye hour our** tickets."

8. They had **mist missed** the show.

9. "Why don't we **meat meet hear here** tomorrow? They will **cell sell** more tickets then," suggested Juan.

10. "Fine," said Scott, "but what can we **dew do right write** now?"

Count 1 point for each correct answer.

_____ My Score

30 Top Score

Extension
Write three sentences using the homophones studied in this lesson. Have a partner choose the correct word.

Multiple-Meaning Words

Rule	Example
Multiple-meaning words are words that have the same spelling and pronunciation but have more than one meaning and may be different parts of speech in different situations.	**gorge** **Noun:** a deep, narrow valley with steep sides **Verb:** to eat greedily

Write the letter of the correct definition of *fix* in each blank.

a. (noun) a position of difficulty or embarrassment

b. (noun) a determination of one's position

c. (noun) something that fixes or restores

d. (verb) to mend or repair

e. (verb) to prepare

1. The divers got a _____ on the wreck of the *Titanic*.

2. When Ashley left her lunch money at home, she was in a terrible _____.

3. The art teacher will _____ my broken vase.

4. The chef will _____ lunch.

5. The tire patch was just a quick _____.

6. The aspirin was a great _____ for my headache.

7. We made a _____ of our location on the chart.

8. May I _____ you a sandwich?

9. Telling lies can get you in a _____.

10. Please, _____ this rip in my shirt.

Count 1 point for each correct answer.

_____ **My Score**

10 Top Score

Extension
Find a word in the dictionary that is two different parts of speech. Write two sentences, one for each part of speech for the word.

Lesson 59

Prefixes, Suffixes, and Roots

Rule	Example
You can often figure out the meaning of a word you do not know by looking at its parts. The main part of a word is called its **root.** For example, the root **audio** means "hear."	**audience** a group that hears a performance **auditory nerve** a nerve that sends sound from the ear to the brain
Prefixes are word parts added to the beginning of a root that change its meaning.	**coworker** a person one works with **cowrite** to write together
Suffixes are word parts added to the end of a root that change its meaning.	**fearful** full of fear **spoonful** amount that fills a spoon

Use the following roots, prefixes, and suffixes to make words. Use at least one root, prefix, or suffix from the chart in each word you write.

Prefixes	Roots	Suffixes
bi-	agri	-able, -ible
inter-	astro	-al
non-	cent	-ant
para-	cycl	-ar
post-	di	-dom
pre-	fix	-ese
re-	gen	-hood
trans-	phile	-ment

Example _____ observant _____

1. _____

2. _____

3. _____

4. _____

5. _____

6. _____

7. _____

8. _____

9. _____

10. _____

Count 1 point for each correct answer.

_____ **My Score**

10 Top Score

Extension
Look in the dictionary for a word that you do not know. Write its parts and their definitions.

77

Lesson **60**

Analogies

An **analogy** compares two pairs of words. The relationship between the two words in the first pair is the same as the relationship between the words in the second pair.

Rule

One kind of analogy shows the relationship between **synonyms**.

Another kind of analogy shows the relationship between **antonyms**.

A third kind of analogy involves one term describing something about the other term.

Example

Happy is to **glad** as **sad** is to **downcast**.

Hard is to **soft** as **friends** are to **enemies**.

Dog is to **bark** as **cat** is to **meow**.

Circle the word that best completes the analogy.

1. Smooth is to flat as rough is to **tough uneven**.

2. Wet is to dry as fast is to **slow race**.

3. Captain is to lead as tutor is to **class teach**.

4. Car is to road as train is to **ticket track**.

5. Clue is to hint as funny is to **comical grin**.

6. Snow is to white as sapphire is to **jewel ring**.

7. Tame is to wild as worst is to **bad best**.

8. Higher is to lower as senior is to **classmate junior**.

9. Steel is to strong as glass is to **fragile window**.

10. Tired is to weary as answer is to **question reply**.

Count 1 point for each correct answer.

_____ My Score
10 Top Score

Extension
Write an analogy using one of the three kinds of analogies learned in this lesson.

78

Review Lessons 55–60

- **Match the type of context clue with the sentence in which it is used.**

  a. comparison   b. cause and effect   c. definition

1. _____ Max planted a hedge of bushes alongside the house because he likes a boundary between the neighbors and himself.

2. _____ Ireland has interesting loughs, which are bays or inlets of the sea.

3. _____ My little sister joked that our dog is invisible, but I could see it, so I knew she was teasing.

| jump | previous | rude | courteous |

- **Write a synonym for the word in parentheses. Use words from the list above.**

4. We worked together to review the _____ day's work. (earlier)

5. Our parents taught us to be _____. (thoughtful)

- **Write an antonym for the bold word. Use words from the list above.**

6. Tyler is **polite**, but his brother Tim is _____.

7. Please, don't **fall** when you _____ on the trampoline.

- **Circle the correct word.**

8. Juan has **to too two** tickets for **their there they're** play.

9. **"Hear Here** are **your you're** programs," said the usher.

10. "I'd like **to too two buy by bye** something to drink," said Juan.

- **Circle the word that best completes the analogy.**

11. Big is to large as small is to **tiny huge.**

12. Hot is to cold as light is to **bright dark.**

Count 1 point for each correct answer.

_____ **My Score**
15 Top Score

Cumulative Review Units 1–4

•Unit 1 **Circle each pronoun.**

1. Nebraska has its capital in Lincoln.

2. Is your birthplace in New Hampshire?

3. Can you tell them that I called?

•Unit 1 **Circle the direct object.**

4. We celebrate Thanksgiving in November.

5. My mother gave me a photograph of her parents.

6. Cedric rode his bike to the river.

•Unit 1 **Write the contractions of these words.**

7. I am _____   9. they are _____

8. let us _____   10. we have _____

•Unit 2 **Write the correct form of the verb in parentheses.**

11. Jesse Owens _____ one of the greatest athletes of all time. (is)

12. He _____ four gold medals at the 1936 Olympics. (win)

•Unit 2 **Revise this sentence to correct the dangling participle.**

13. Lying under the refrigerator, I saw my missing keys.

_____

•Unit 3 **Circle each letter that should be a capital.**

14. In 1777, the articles of confederation were ratified by new hampshire, massachusetts, rhode island, connecticut, new york, new jersey, pennsylvania, delaware, virginia, north carolina, south carolina, georgia, and maryland.

•Unit 3 **Circle the subordinate clause. Add the comma.**

15. If you can come to the party bring chips.

Cumulative Review

•Unit 4   Write a synonym for the word in parentheses. Use words from the list.

friendly   petite   immature

16. Please, don't act so _____. (childish)

•Unit 4   Write an antonym for the word in bold type. Use words from the list above.

17. My grandmother is not **big;** she is very _____.

18. Why can't you look _____ instead of **stern?**

•Unit 4   Circle the correct word.

19. **Hear   Here** are **you're   your** shoes.

20. I can **meat   meet** you at **fore   four.**

21. The test was **sew   so** easy.

•Unit 4   Use the following roots, prefixes, and suffixes to make words. Use at least one root, prefix, or suffix from the chart in each word you write.

Prefixes	Roots	Suffixes
anti-	am	-ar
dis-	eu	-fy
peri-	mon	-ness

22. _____   24. _____

23. _____   25. _____

Count 1 point for each correct answer.

_____ **My Score**
50 Top Score

UNIT 4: Vocabulary

Name _____

UNIT 4 Inventory

Use context clues to figure out the meaning of the bold word. Write the meaning. *Lesson 55*

1. While in the army, my dad said he ate in the **mess hall** with the other servicemen.

   _____

   _____

2. Why do you **procrastinate?** Why can't you do your work right away?

   _____

   _____

Circle the correct word. *Lesson 57*

3. **Their There They're** is someone at the door **for four** you.

4. **Their There They're waiting weighting** for an answer.

5. Have you **read red you're your** lesson?

6. Please, **dew do** the problems on the **right write**.

7. I have the **flew flu.**

8. I have **been bin** in the house for a **weak week.**

9. Are **ewe you to too two** sick to **read reed?**

Use the following roots, prefixes, and suffixes to make words. Use at least one root, prefix, or suffix from the chart in each word you write. *Lesson 59*

Prefixes	Roots	Suffixes
contra-	audio	-oy
mis-	grat	-hood
pro-	poly	-ous

10. _____

11. _____

12. _____

13. _____

14. _____

15. _____

Circle the word that best completes the analogy.

16. Oral is to spoken as example is to **illustration exact.**

17. Hard is to soft as better is to **worse bad.**

18. Carpenter is to hammer as writer is to **book pencil.**

Lesson 61

Reference Skills

Using a Dictionary

Rule	Example
Alphabetize words and names by comparing letter by letter.	**sel**dom **sem**icolon **ser**vice
Guide words at the top of the page show the first and last entry words on the page.	The word **trail** has the guide words **trade-off** and **train** in some dictionaries.
The **pronunciation** is given after the entry word. The **part of speech** of the word is listed after the pronunciation. The plural-form **spelling** of an irregular noun is given after the part of speech. If the word has more than one **meaning,** each meaning is numbered.	pronunciation part of speech meaning **reply** \ri plī´\ vb 1: to respond in words or writing 2: to do something in response — replies second meaning irregular plural spelling

List these words in alphabetical order.

initial   rainbow   giraffe   enemy   poem   parade   puzzle

1. _____

_____

Write the plural-form spellings for these words.

2. corps _____   4. liberty _____

3. bacterium _____

Count 1 point for each correct answer.

_____ My Score

10 Top Score

Extension
Look in the dictionary and write down the pronunciation, part of speech, definition, and guide words for the word *authority.*

Lesson 62

Using a Table of Contents and an Index

Rule

The **table of contents** appears at the front of the book and is a list of the chapters and subdivisions with their page numbers.

The **index** is an alphabetical list of topics in the book, given with page numbers.

Use the table of contents to answer Questions 1–3. Use the index to answer Questions 4–5.

Table of Contents

Chapter	Page
1 Diets for Good Health	3
2 Threats to Good Health	21
3 Feeding the World's Population	43

Index

Earth, 52, 328–360
Energy
    definition of, 119
    light, 121–125
    mechanical, 134
Evaporation, 374

1. Which chapter might tell how smoking weakens the lungs? _____

2. Which chapter might show the Food Guide Pyramid? _____

3. Which chapter might tell how to protect soil from erosion? _____

4. Which pages would probably tell how a lightbulb works? _____

5. Which pages would probably tell about what happens when a motor is running?

_____

Count 1 point for each correct answer.

_____ My Score
5 Top Score

Extension
Create an index for a chapter of your science or social studies book.

84

Reference Sources

Use **reference sources** to obtain information on a particular topic.

Encyclopedias are designed for quick reference on many subjects.

An **atlas** is a book of maps and statistics about countries, climates, and cultures.

An **almanac** is published annually and is useful for current facts and statistics.

A **thesaurus** is a dictionary of synonyms.

A **book of quotations** has quotations listed by speaker and by subject.

All other **nonfiction** books can be classified as general.

Write the letter of the reference source where you would find these topics.

a. atlas   b. almanac   c. encyclopedia   d. book of quotations

e. general nonfiction   f. thesaurus

1. _____ maps of the 50 states

2. _____ latest world population figures

3. _____ another word for *sonnet*

4. _____ a list of last year's best-selling books

5. _____ person who said, "We have nothing to fear but fear itself."

6. _____ a brief article about Susan B. Anthony

7. _____ a book on how to build a go-cart

8. _____ the history and uses of the Danube River

9. _____ camping and woodcrafts

10. _____ person who said, "May the Force be with you!"

Count 1 point for each correct answer.

_____ **My Score**
10 Top Score

Extension
Write a short report describing what is in a particular reference book in your library.

Organizing Information: Webs

Rule

Using a **web** is a way of organizing information. The **main idea** should be in the center with the **subtopics** going outward. **Additional details** go outward from the subtopics.

Example

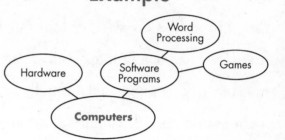

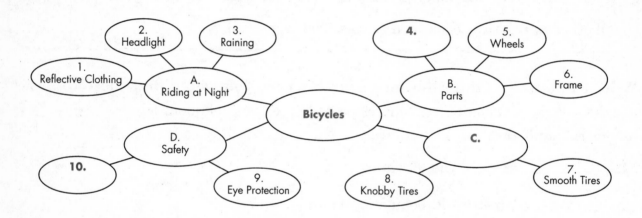

Based on the web, circle the letter that best answers the following questions.

1. Which of these should go in circle C?

   a. Types of Tires   b. Wheels

2. Which of these should go in circle 4?

   a. Chain   b. Eye Protection

3. Which of these should go in circle 10?

   a. Chain   b. Helmet

4. Which idea in the web does not belong?

   a. 1   b. 3

5. If you wanted to add to circle B, which of these would be best?

   a. Warm Jacket   b. Seat

Count 1 point for each correct answer.

_____ **My Score**

5 Top Score

Extension

From a section in your science or social studies book, create a web.

86

Tables

> ## Rule
> A **table** can present much information in a small amount of space. Information is listed in rows and columns.

Highest Altitude

Continent	Highest Point	Elevation (feet)	Country
Asia	Mount Everest	29,028	Nepal/Tibet
South America	Mount Aconcagua	22,834	Argentina
North America	Mount McKinley	20,320	United States
Africa	Mount Kilimanjaro	19,340	Tanzania
Europe	Mont Blanc	15,771	France/Italy
Australia	Mount Kosciusko	7,310	Australia

Based on the table above, answer these questions.

1. The mountain with the highest point is _____.

2. The highest point in Tanzania is _____.

3. The mountain peak closest to 22,000 feet high is _____.

4. Mount Kosciusko is located in which country? _____

5. The elevation of Mont Blanc is _____.

Count 1 point for each correct answer.

_____ **My Score**
5 Top Score

Extension
Find a table in one of your subject books. Take turns asking a partner questions about the table.

Conducting Research

Rule

Summarize on **note cards** important facts, ideas, and opinions from your research. The information on a note card should be about a single topic. Use **key words** to help you organize your material. Record the author's name, source title, and the page number of the information. Put quotation marks around the exact words that you wish to quote.

Example

> key word
>
> **Population**
> "All oak trees in a front yard, all humans in the world, and all bats in a cave make up different populations."
> ***Science for Living,***
> **Mark Harris, page 48**

Energy from the sun strikes Earth every day. Energy produced on the sun travels to Earth in about eight minutes. Always use sunscreen. Energy from the sun is called solar energy.

"The solar energy that strikes the U. S. each day is greater than the energy in 22 million barrels of crude oil."

David Armstrong, p. 24.

Use the information above to answer the questions.

1. What is the topic of this information?
   a. crude oil
   b. energy from the sun

2. What key words would you use for this note card?
   a. Sun and Light   b. Solar Energy

3. Does this note card include a direct quotation?
   a. yes   b. no

4. Which sentence does not belong on this note card?
   a. You should always use sunscreen.
   b. Energy produced on the sun travels to Earth in about eight minutes.

5. What information is missing from this note card?
   a. chapter title
   b. source title

Count 1 point for each correct answer.

_____ **My Score**

5 Top Score

Extension
Research and write note cards for a short paper on any topic you wish.

Review Lessons 61–66

- **Alphabetize these words by writing the correct number for each word.**

  _____ pitcher   _____ woolen   _____ capital   _____ attic

- **Write the letter of the reference source where you would find these topics.**

  a. a dictionary   b. an almanac   c. an atlas

  1. _____ a list of the current United States senators

  2. _____ the pronunciation of *equanimity*

  3. _____ the average yearly precipitation of India

- **Based on the web, answer these questions.**

  4. _____ Which of these should go in circle 2?
     a. Future of Jasper   b. Limestone

  5. _____ Which of these should go in circle D?
     a. Daily life   b. Other industries

  6. Which circle would probably tell about the founding of Jasper?
     a. A   b. B

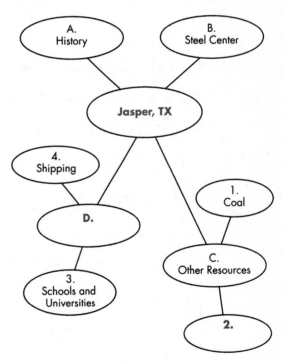

Count 1 point for each correct answer.

_____ **My Score**
10 Top Score

Name _____

•Unit 1 **Above each word write the word's part of speech. Use *n* for *noun*, *v* for *verb*, *pron* for *pronoun*, *adj* for *adjective*, *adv* for *adverb*, *prep* for *preposition*, *conj* for *conjunction*, and *i* for *interjection*.**

Marie Antoinette was born in Austria. She was the daughter of Austrian rulers Marie Theresa and Francis I. After her marriage to King Louis XVI of France, she was hated by an anti-Austrian group in the French court. She often sought the advice of the Austrian ambassador to France, so the French people suspected she was spying on France for her home country. After the French Revolution began, she secretly urged the Austrians' declaration of war on France.

•Unit 2 **Write the contractions of these words.**

1. it is _____   2. you are _____

Cross out the pronouns that are not needed.

3. The nations of the world they face many threats to the environment.

4. In 1997, Earth Summit II it was held to discuss environmental issues.

5. The delegates they agreed that international cooperation is needed.

Write the correct form of the verb in parentheses.

6. Some delegates _____ that industrial nations, which _____ free of environmental regulations when they _____ their own industries, were being unfair to developing nations. (feel) (are) (build)

Circle the word that best completes the analogy.

7. Funny is to comical as tired is to **road weary.**

8. Band is to march as teacher is to **teach chalk.**

•Unit 3 **Insert commas and semicolons where needed.**

9. The field events included races the high jump the long jump pole vaulting shot putting and discus throwing.

Cumulative Review

10. The teams came from three schools: Tempe High School, Tempe Arizona Madison High School, Madison Wisconsin and Traverse Bay High School, Traverse Bay Michigan.

Circle the appositive and underline the noun that is identified or explained.

11. The shot, a heavy, cannonlike ball, is held in one hand and pushed away from the body.

tame	oral	soft	illustration

•Unit 4 **Write a synonym for the word in parentheses. Use words from the list above.**

12. Miguel, it's your turn to give your _____ report. (spoken)

13. Please, show an _____ for your point. (example)

Write an antonym for the word in bold type. Use words from the list above.

14. Did the pilot make a **hard** landing or a _____ landing?

15. Do you like _____ animals or **wild** animals?

•Unit 5 **List these words in alphabetical order.**

16. pony _____   18. pole _____

17. picture _____   19. paper _____

Write the reference source where you would find these topics.

20. a list of celebrities and entertainers _____

21. a synonym for *hero* _____

22. person who said "A penny saved is a penny earned." _____

Count 1 point for each correct answer.   _____ My Score
                                                                    105 Top Score

Name _____

UNIT 5 Inventory

Using a dictionary, show the guide words, pronunciation (syllables and marks), and part of speech for the word *island*.
Lesson 61

1. island

_____

_____

_____

Use the index to answer Questions 2–5.
Lesson 62

South Vietnam, 140–144

Southwest, United States

    climate of, 38–41

    missions in, 98–101

    Native Americans in, 64–71

Space shuttle, 256–257

2. Which pages would probably tell about the yearly precipitation of Texas? _____

3. Which pages would probably tell about the Navajo and Hopi? _____

4. Which pages would probably tell about Father Junipero Serra?

_____

5. Which pages would probably tell about the space program? _____

Write the letter of the reference source where you would find these topics.
Lesson 63

a. an almanac   b. a thesaurus
c. a dictionary

6. _____ the population of Louisiana

7. _____ the definition of *pretentious*

8. _____ a synonym for *overlook*

9. _____ a list of this century's volcanic eruptions

10. _____ an antonym for *smile*

Use the table to answer Questions 11–13.
Lesson 65

European Countries

Country	Population (in millions)	Geographic Area (in thousands)
France	58	211 sq. miles
Germany	82	137 sq. miles
Italy	56	116 sq. miles
Spain	39	194 sq. miles

11. _____ Which country has the largest population?

    a. France   b. Germany
    c. Italy   d. Spain

12. _____ Which two countries have geographic areas less than 150,000 square miles?

    a. France and Spain
    b. France and Italy
    c. Germany and Italy
    d. Italy and Spain

13. _____ Which country has a population of 58 million?

    a. France   b. Germany
    c. Italy   d. Spain

Count 1 point for each correct answer.

_____ My Score
15 Top Score

Writing Structure ## Topic Sentences

Rule	Example
The **topic sentence** of a paragraph tells what the paragraph is about. A topic sentence can be at the beginning or the end of a paragraph.	<u>Most Europeans did not believe that the fighting of World War I would last long.</u> However, they were wrong. In the end, the fighting dragged on for four years, and millions died.

Underline the topic sentence in each of these paragraphs.

Weapons took a terrible toll on human lives. For example, during the Battle of the Somme, which lasted for less than five months in 1916, a combined total of 1 million French, British, and German soldiers lost their lives.

The army needed weapons, food, clothing, and fuel. Many factories worked overtime. With so many men fighting in the war, jobs that had been closed to women and African Americans became available to them for the first time. Americans on the home front made great contributions to the war effort.

Write a topic sentence for each topic below as if you were using it to begin a paragraph on that topic.

1. Tropical plants

   _____

2. The zoo

   _____

3. Breakfast foods

   _____

Count 1 point for each correct answer.

_____ **My Score**

5 Top Score

Extension
Review some of your past writing assignments. Underline the topic sentence in each piece.

Lesson 68

Supporting Sentences

Rule	Example
Supporting sentences provide supporting details, facts and statistics, examples, and incidents for the topic sentence. This paragraph has supporting sentences that give examples.	The amazing feats of master chess players show that real expertise requires a unique talent, a special kind of imagination, and memory. <u>Many champions have been able to play 100 good opponents at the same time. Even more extraordinary is the ability of masters to play "blindfold" chess in which they are told their opponent's moves by an umpire and go on to report their own moves without ever seeing the board.</u>

Write a paragraph with a topic sentence and four supporting sentences. Make sure the supporting sentences provide supporting details, facts and statistics, examples, and incidents for the topic sentence.

_____

_____

_____

_____

_____

_____

_____

Count 1 point for
each correct answer.

_____ **My Score**
5 Top Score

Extension
Find examples of the different types of supporting sentences—details, facts, examples, incidents. Share them with the class.

Lesson **69**

Staying on Topic and Logical Order

Rule	Example
A paragraph is made of sentences telling about one topic or idea. Each sentence should tell or ask something about the paragraph topic. The sentences should be arranged to tell things in the order in which they happen.	not on topic Heat can make liquids boil. I burned myself on the stove. When water boils, it turns into a gas. Solid, liquid, and gas are three states of matter.

Use the paragraph to answer the questions.

1 Use scissors to cut off the small end of a balloon. 2 I like to buy my balloons at the car wash. 3 Observe what happens. 4 Be careful so the balloon does not break. 5 Put a rubber band around the can to hold the balloon in place. 6 _____ 7 Stretch the balloon over the open end of the coffee can.

1. Which two sentences should be switched in order? _____
   a. 1 and 3   b. 2 and 7   c. 3 and 7

2. Which sentence best fits the blank in the paragraph? _____
   a. Check the rubber band for a tight fit.
   b. Tap your drum with the eraser end of the pencil.

3. Which sentence does not belong? _____
   a. 2   b. 3   c. 5

4. Choose the best first sentence for the paragraph. _____
   a. Try to find a pencil with an eraser for this activity.
   b. The following is an activity to help you see and hear sound waves.

5. Choose the best last sentence for the paragraph. _____
   a. Record what you see.
   b. Be careful with the rubber band.

Extension
Tell a story about a time you found yourself in a funny situation. Tell things in the correct order.

Count 1 point for each correct answer.

_____ **My Score**
5 Top Score

Paragraphing

The **introductory paragraph** of a composition presents the main idea.

The **body paragraphs** support the main idea. Each new idea in the body must be in a separate paragraph. The body paragraphs need to be in a logical order. You can put them in order of how the events happened, order of importance, or simple to complex.

The **concluding paragraph** summarizes the information in the body paragraphs.

Write in the blanks the best order of the paragraphs below.

1. _____ 2. _____ 3. _____ 4. _____ 5. _____

A. Thomas Jefferson, who was from the South, thought the capital should be in one of the southern states. Leaders from the North thought Boston or New York would be a good choice.

B. After the Revolutionary War, the leaders of the United States had trouble deciding where to build a capital city for the new country. Everyone had different ideas on the location for the capital.

C. In 1790, President George Washington signed an Act of Congress that established the nation's capital. He helped choose the site for the new presidential home, and construction began.

D. Although George Washington helped choose the site for the White House, he never lived there. In 1800, President John Adams and his wife, Abigail, became the first presidential family to live in the White House.

E. Finally, members of Congress agreed that the capital should not be in any one state. Instead, it should be separate and belong to all the people of the country.

Count 1 point for each correct answer.

_____ My Score
5 Top Score

Extension
Choose a chapter in one of your subject books. Point out to the class examples of logical paragraph order.

Lesson 71

Paragraphing Quotations

Rule	Example
In writing conversation, make a new paragraph each time the speaker changes.	"There's nothing to do today," Shawn complained. "Let's stay home and bake cookies," April suggested. "That sounds great!" Mark replied.
When proofreading, make the paragraph mark ¶ when you need to make a new paragraph on your final paper.	"Look! I have a loose tooth!" Jacob said to LeAnn.¶"Does it hurt?" asked LeAnn.

Put in the paragraph marks for additional paragraphs, quotation marks, and one missing comma.

On Saturday morning, Nicole and Paul slowly walked down the street toward the roller rink. As they walked, they chatted about the skating party. These two weeks have gone by so quickly, said Nicole. Yes, agreed Paul, they really have. I'm glad we thought of this skating party, said Nicole, especially since the rink owner is giving our group such a nice discount. What's wrong? asked Nicole, when Paul stopped walking suddenly. I just realized that I left home without a penny, Paul said. You're kidding Nicole said. I wish I were, Paul sighed. I'll have to go home for some money. Don't be silly; you'll miss half the session, Nicole said. I'll lend you whatever money you need.

Count 1 point for each correct answer.

_____ My Score

30 Top Score

Extension

Write a short story that includes conversation between two or people. Divide the story correctly into paragraphs.

Combining Sentences

Rule	Example
Two short sentences can be combined by a connecting word to express a single thought more smoothly.	Marcy carried the rabbit. Eric carried the cage.
If two short sentences are joined with the word *and, or, but,* or *for,* use a comma before the connecting word. When a subordinate clause is used, put a comma after the clause.	Marcy carried the rabbit, **and** Eric carried the cage. **While** Marcy carried the rabbit, Eric carried the cage.

In each group, combine the two sentences to make one sentence. Use the connecting word printed in parentheses. Add a comma if needed.

1. Benjamin Franklin was a scientist. Benjamin Franklin was a diplomat. (and)

   _____

2. Franklin proved that lightning was electricity. He was known in Europe. (because)

   _____

3. He was in Europe. He worked for our country. (while)

   _____

4. He worked in London as an agent for the colonies. He gained the help of France in the cause of American freedom. (and)

   _____

   _____

5. He returned to America. He continued his experiments and inventions. (and)

   _____

Count 1 point for each correct answer.

_____ My Score
5 Top Score

Extension
Find an example of a combined sentence to share with the class.

Name _____

Review Lessons 67–72

- **Underline the topic sentence. Draw a line through sentences that do not tell anything about the topic of the paragraph.**

Election Day is an important day in our country. It takes place on the first Tuesday after the first Monday in November. My birthday is in November. It is the day that national elections are held and is a legal holiday in most states. I live in the state of Ohio. National elections for president and vice-president occur every four years. Voters elect state senators and representatives every two years. I haven't decided which candidate I am going to vote for yet. On the national level, senators run for office every six years. I think I'll be a senator someday. Members of the House of Representatives run every two years.

- **Put in quotation marks and paragraph marks for additional paragraphs.**

Can you believe the New York Yankees team? asked Derek. It was amazing, replied Rene. They won the World Series for the 25th time, said Derek. And it was their third back-to-back Series sweep, said Rene. Do you think any team will ever have such an exciting season? asked Derek.

- **Combine the two sentences to make one sentence. Use the connecting word printed in parentheses.**

Many people watch soccer in Europe. Baseball is more popular in the United States. (but)

_____

_____

•Lessons 67, 69

•Lesson 71

•Lesson 72

Count 1 point for
each correct answer.

_____ My Score
20 Top Score

Cumulative Review   Units 1–6

•Unit 1   **Above each word write the word's part of speech. Use *n* for *noun, v* for *verb, pron* for *pronoun, adj* for *adjective, adv* for *adverb, prep* for *preposition, conj* for *conjunction,* and *i* for *interjection.***

The cliff dwellings at Mesa Verde were unknown for nearly 600 years.

Then a rancher saw the pueblos while looking for lost cattle on a Ute

reservation. Theodore Roosevelt made Mesa Verde a national park.

•Unit 2   **Circle the correct word.**

   1. **You're Your**   drawing is here.

   2. I know **who's whose**   CD that is.

   3. **It's Its**   Jamie's CD.

Write the correct form of the verb in parentheses.

   4. My brother _____ the class turtle for the weekend. (bring)

   5. It _____ crickets. (eat)

Revise the sentence to correct the dangling modifier.

   6. Having recovered from his illness, his mother sent him to school.

_____

•Unit 3   **Circle each letter that should be a capital. Place periods where needed.**

   7. Are your initials trm?

   8. Yes, aunt alice and i went to egypt in march.

   9. May i go to nurse abbott's office?

Circle the subordinate clause. Add the comma.

  10. After you complete your statue put away all the supplies.

Circle the appositive and underline the noun that is identified or explained by the appositive.

  11. Sandy, our Airedale, is a dog with personality.

Cumulative Review

•Unit 4   Use context clues to figure out the antonym of the bold word.

12. "I do not **shrink** from this responsibility; I welcome it," said President John F. Kennedy.

_____

Use the following roots, prefixes, and suffixes to make words. Use at least one root, prefix, or suffix from the chart in each word you write.

Prefixes	Roots	Suffixes
de-	geo	-age
hyper-	ject	-ary
pro-	port	-ful

13. _____   **15.** _____

14. _____   **16.** _____

•Unit 5   Write this word to show the guide words, pronunciation (syllables and marks), and part of speech.

17. lend

_____

_____

_____

•Unit 6   Write a topic sentence for *summer*.

_____

_____

_____

Count 1 point for each correct answer.   _____ My Score
                                                          65 Top Score

UNIT 6: Writing Structure   **101**

UNIT 6 Inventory

Underline the topic sentence. Draw a line through sentences that do not tell anything about the topic of the paragraph.
Lessons 67, 69

   People all over the world have flown kites for thousands of years. Kites made of leaves were used by many cultures. I had a red kite once. One example is the Polynesian fishing kite, which was used to snare fish swimming near the water's surface. Have you ever been fishing? I used a sheet to make a tail for my kite. Benjamin Franklin used a flat kite in his electricity experiment. Then the box kite was invented in 1893. The United States Weather Bureau used box kites in the early 1900s to record weather conditions. I wonder what the weather will be tomorrow. The Wright brothers used box kites in tests that led to their invention of the airplane.

Use the connecting word in parentheses to combine the sentences.
Lesson 72

1. In 1999, Michael Jordan retired. In 1999, Wayne Gretzky retired. In 1999, Steffi Graf retired. (and)

   _____

   _____

   _____

2. The United States soccer team won its second World Cup. Women's soccer got a huge boost in the United States. (when)

   _____

   _____

   _____

   _____

3. Soccer is popular in the United States. Baseball is more popular. (but)

   _____

   _____

4. On the final day of the Ryder Cup, the American golfers trailed. They managed to win. (but)

   _____

   _____

   _____

5. Justin Leonard sank a 45-foot putt. They won. (after)

   _____

   _____

   _____

Count 1 point for each correct answer.

_____ **My Score**

10 Top Score

Review List

Mechanics

Use a **capital letter** for the word *I* and for each initial of a name.

Use a **capital letter** to begin

1. the first word of a sentence
2. each name of a person or pet
3. each word in a particular person, place, thing, or idea
4. the name of a relative (*Mother, Uncle*) when used as or with a name but not with the words *my, our, your, his, her,* or *their*
5. a title of respect, such as *Dr., Mr., Miss, Mrs.,* or *Ms.*
6. each word in a day, a month, or a holiday
7. the first word and every important word in the title of a story, a book, a magazine, a play, a poem, or a song
8. the first word and every important word in the greeting and the first word of the closing in a letter
9. the name of a country or nationality
10. the first word of a direct quotation

Use an **apostrophe**

1. in a contraction where letters are left out
2. in a noun with **-s** to show possession

Use a **semicolon**

1. between two sentences joined by words such as *therefore, however,* and *for example*
2. to separate the items in a series when the items contain commas

Use a **comma**

1. between the name of a city and its state (and after the state if the city and state are used in a sentence)
2. between a day of the month and the year (and after the year if the month, day, and year are used in a sentence)
3. after the greeting and closing of a friendly letter
4. in a series after each word or group of words except the last
5. to separate the name of a person spoken to from the rest of the sentence
6. to separate the words *yes* and *no* when they are used as part of an answer
7. to set off a direct quotation from the rest of a sentence
8. after the part of a sentence that begins with a connecting word if that part comes at the beginning of the sentence
9. before a coordinating conjunction (such as *and, but,* or *for*)

Use a **colon** after the greeting of a business letter.

Quotation Marks

1. Use **quotation marks** to enclose a direct quotation.
2. When writing a conversation, put a comma inside the **quotation mark** to separate the quotation from the rest of the sentence. Periods, question marks, and exclamation marks should be placed inside the **quotation mark** as well.
3. Use **quotation marks** to enclose the title of a song, a poem, or a story if the title is used in a sentence.

Underline or italicize the title of a book when it is used in a sentence.

Grammar and Usage

Verbs

1. With singular nouns and with *he, she,* or *it,* use *is, isn't, was, wasn't, has, hasn't, doesn't.*
2. With plural nouns and with *they* or *you,* use *are, aren't, were, weren't, don't, have, haven't.*

Review List

3. Use **is** and **was** with **there** when you speak of one person or thing; use **are** and **were** with **there** when you speak of more than one person or thing.

4. Use **sit** to mean "to rest" and **set** to mean "to place."

5. Use **lie** to mean "to rest" or "to recline" and **lay** to mean "to place" or "to put."

6. Use **may** in asking or giving permission and **can** in expressing ability to do something.

Nouns

1. **Irregular plural nouns** have unique spellings (*man, men; deer, deer*). Use a dictionary to check if you are unsure.

2. To show **possession** in a singular noun and in a plural noun that does not end in **-s**, add an apostrophe and **-s** (*dog, dog's; oxen, oxen's*). For a plural noun that ends in **-s**, add only an apostrophe (*boys, boys'*).

Pronouns

1. Use **this, that, these,** and **those** to point out, and **them** to stand for the names of persons or things. Never use **them** as an adjective.

2. Always **speak of yourself last** when you speak of yourself and others together.

3. **Possessive pronouns** take the place of possessive nouns. **My, your, his, her, its, our, your,** and **their** are used before a noun. **Mine, your, his, hers, its, ours, yours,** and **theirs** are used alone.

4. Use **who** for subjects (**Who** was at the door?) and **whom** for objects (**Whom** did you see?).

Vocabulary

Synonyms are words that are similar in meaning, and **antonyms** are words that are opposite in meaning.

Homophones

1. Use **their** to mean "belonging to them"; **there** to mean "in that place" or at the beginning of a sentence with **is, are, was,** or **were;** and **they're** as the contraction of **they are.**

2. Use **too** to mean "more than enough" or "also," **two** to mean the number 2, and **to** to name an action or with a noun to show motion toward.

3. Use **its** as a possessive pronoun and **it's** as a contraction of **it is.**

Adjectives

1. An **adjective** describes, points out, or numbers a noun or pronoun.

2. Use **an** before a word beginning with a vowel sound, and **a** before a word beginning with a consonant sound.

3. **Comparative adjectives** show greater or smaller, usually by adding **-er** (*large, larger; good, better*).

4. **Superlative adjectives** show greatest or smallest, usually by adding **-est** (*large, largest; good, best*).

5. **Good** and **bad** are **adjectives. Badly** and **well** are **adverbs. Well** may also be used as an adjective to mean "satisfactory" or "in good health."

Adverbs

1. An **adverb** is used with a verb to tell how, when, where, or to what extent.

2. **Comparative adverbs** compare two actions, often by adding **more** or **less** (*fast, faster; often, more often*).

3. **Superlative adverbs** compare three or more actions, often by adding **most** or **least** (*fast, fastest; often, most often*).

A **conjunction** (such as **and, but, because, while,** or **if**) is a word that connects words or groups of words.

A **preposition** (such as **at, before, from, for, to, under,** or **with**) shows the relationship of a noun to another word in a sentence.

United States Postal Service
State Abbreviations

Alabama	AL	Montana	MT
Alaska	AK	Nebraska	NE
Arizona	AZ	Nevada	NV
Arkansas	AR	New Hampshire	NH
California	CA	New Jersey	NJ
Colorado	CO	New Mexico	NM
Connecticut	CT	New York	NY
Delaware	DE	North Carolina	NC
District of Columbia	DC	North Dakota	ND
Florida	FL	Ohio	OH
Georgia	GA	Oklahoma	OK
Hawaii	HI	Oregon	OR
Idaho	ID	Pennsylvania	PA
Illinois	IL	Rhode Island	RI
Indiana	IN	South Carolina	SC
Iowa	IA	South Dakota	SD
Kansas	KS	Tennessee	TN
Kentucky	KY	Texas	TX
Louisiana	LA	Utah	UT
Maine	ME	Vermont	VT
Maryland	MD	Virginia	VA
Massachusetts	MA	Washington	WA
Michigan	MI	West Virginia	WV
Minnesota	MN	Wisconsin	WI
Mississippi	MS	Wyoming	WY
Missouri	MO		